PRAISE FOR *CLOUT*

"I never thought of myself as a leader until one day my small ministry wasn't so small any longer. Since the people I lead deserve to be led well, I knew I had to get intentional about reading great books to equip me. *Clout* is a wonderful resource for learning to lead from a place of security and surrender. Jenni helped me understand the necessary balance between these two principles so I can walk confidently in the clout entrusted to me and honor God in the process."

—LYSA TERKEURST, *NEW YORK TIMES* BEST-SELLING
AUTHOR AND PRESIDENT OF PROVERBS 31 MINISTRIES

"You were made to matter. Jenni Catron embodies, lives, and breathes this great truth. *Clout* is a deeply honest, personal, thoughtful, activist call that will provoke growth where you most need it, and impact where you most hunger for it."

—JOHN ORTBERG, SENIOR PASTOR OF MENLO PARK
PRESBYTERIAN CHURCH; AUTHOR OF *WHO IS THIS MAN?*

"God has given Jenni Catron a voice, a heart, and a message for this moment. As our understanding of leadership begins to shift in our culture and in the church, this is a timely call to every man, woman, and child to step into their calling and shine."

—SHEILA WALSH, AUTHOR OF *THE STORM INSIDE*

"Jenni's leadership has been invaluable to me and our church. If you've ever bought into the lie that you don't have what it takes and it's kept you from fully living out your purpose, then you need to read this book. Jenni will not only help you identify what's been holding you back, she'll lead you on a life-changing journey to discover and live out your God-given influence."

—PETE WILSON, SENIOR PASTOR, CROSS POINT
CHURCH; AUTHOR OF *PLAN B* AND *LET HOPE IN*

"Jenni Catron has the uncanny ability to get to the heart of the matter when it comes to leadership. How will you invest your influence? This book brings you to a great understanding of what having clout means and how you can leverage it in your everyday leadership. If you are a leader who wants to lead with their God-given best, you can't miss *Clout*."

—SHERRY SURRATT, CEO AND PRESIDENT, MOPS, INTERNATIONAL

"Jenni Catron transforms the secular concept of *Clout* into a Christ-anchored advantage for Christians. Challenging and practical, this work explores the subtle sins that limit God's ability to use us and then provides the biblical truth that frees us to influence the world in His strength and power. Catron has written a timely and essential study for any Christian called to lead in a time such as this."

—TAMI HEIM, PRESIDENT AND CEO OF
CHRISTIAN LEADERSHIP ALLIANCE

"What can I say—Jenni's got a gift! I am so excited she wrote this book. Her stories are honest and real and her perspective is fresh and sound. Inside this book is the power to transform teams in churches, non-profits and businesses alike. Jenni's approach to leadership and influence is spot on for a new generation of leaders emerging today."

—MATT KELLER, AUTHOR OF *GOD OF THE
UNDERDOGS*, @MATTHEWKELLER

"*Clout* is the book that every developing leader not only needs to read, but WANTS to read. Jenni Catron gives clear direction on how to leverage your influence, no matter the size, for the good of others and the glory of God."

—ANNIE DOWNS, AUTHOR OF
SPEAK LOVE AND PERFECTLY UNIQUE

"Finally, a book that redeems the word *clout* and emboldens every Christian to influence others with lasting impact."

—FRANK VIOLA, AUTHOR OF *GOD'S FAVORITE
PLACE ON EARTH*, FRANKVIOLA.ORG

"Jenni Catron writes with distinctive style, refreshing candor and is a great storyteller! In her new book, *Clout*, Jenni delivers 'Clout Killers' we all face and 'Clout Cultivators' that will add significant value to your leadership. This book gives strong practical wisdom with a positive perspective on how to overcome and rise up to your leadership potential!"

—DAN REILAND, EXECUTIVE PASTOR,
12STONE CHURCH

"I'm so honored to recommend this book to anyone who is facing the gap between their purpose and their present circumstance. Jenni has the rare gift of combining solid, biblical, business-savvy advice while being extremely transparent and warm. She has the integrity and intelligence to back it up, and the heart to pass it along to even those who can't imagine they'll reach their potential. On a personal level, I've had the honor of working alongside her and seeing the way she lives out every bit of what she teaches; she's steady, loyal, strong, and just flat-out likable. She's poured herself into words that will change the way you understand and respond to the Lord's calling, and I hope you'll soak them up and pass them along. She's a treasure to me and I know she will be to you as well."

—ANGIE SMITH, BEST-SELLING AUTHOR OF *MENDED*,
I WILL CARRY YOU, AND *WHAT WOMEN FEAR*

"#FistBump to Jenni Catron for using her *Clout* to help the rest of us find ours. Her field guide to discovering your point of maximum impact in the world offers relatable stories and reliable insight. . . . and, true to its name, *Clout* pulls no punches in motivating readers to get up and tap into their God-given influence."

—@SCOTTWILLIAMS, CHURCH GROWTH/LEADERSHIP
CONSULTANT AND STRATEGIST AT NXT LEVEL SOLUTIONS;
AUTHOR OF *CHURCH DIVERSITY* AND *GO BIG*

"In *Clout*, Jenni Catron deftly captures how we can confidently live out God's design and purpose for our lives. Sprinkled with personal stories and supported with biblical insight, Jenni's writing will encourage your heart. I highly recommend *Clout* for anyone looking to maximize their Kingdom impact and live a joy-filled life."

—Dr. Charles Stone, lead pastor, West Park Church, London, England, and Ontario, Canada; author of *People-Pleasing Pastors: Avoiding the Pitfalls of Approval-Motivated Leadership*

"I tried to think of a category of person this book wouldn't help—I came up empty. Whether a seasoned leader, a college student, a CEO, or a stay-at-home mom—*Clout* has practical handles for anyone who wants to leverage their influence."

—Tim Stevens, executive pastor, Granger Community Church; author of *Vision: Lost and Found*

"Whether we admit it or not, we *all* have clout. There are people in our lives who we influence. How we choose to steward that influence, though, will change the trajectory of our lives *and* the people around us. Through stories and practical next steps, Jenni does a masterful job of challenging us to consider how we will discover and unleash our God-given clout."

—Tony Morgan, author, consultant, leadership coach, TheUnstuckGroup.com

"Whether you're a stay-at-home parent or the CEO of a major corporation, you have God-given influence. *Clout* will help you identify, explore, and live in that influence in the way that God intended. Jenni writes with such enthusiasm for your personal growth that you can't help but be encouraged. This is a must-read for anyone with a desire to live fully the calling God has placed on their life."

—Justin Lathrop, Kingdom Connector, author and entrepreneur, www.justinlathrop.com

"Jenni Catron's *Clout* is a must-read for any Christ follower who's ever struggled to find their purpose and passion, or doubted they had anything of value to offer to God's work in the world. With a style that's accessible, straightforward, practical, and most of all, wise, Jenni shows Christ followers how to navigate the often confusing terrain of their own hearts to uncover and unleash their God-given influence in a way that's life-giving—both for them, and world around them."

—MICHAEL WARDEN, LEADERSHIP COACH AND
AUTHOR OF *LEADING WIDE AWAKE: A SPIRITUAL
SURVIVAL GUIDE FOR FAITH LEADERS*

CLOUT

CLOUT

DISCOVER AND UNLEASH
YOUR GOD-GIVEN
INFLUENCE

JENNI CATRON

NELSON
BOOKS

An Imprint of Thomas Nelson

Published in Nashville, Tennessee, by Nelson Books, an imprint of Thomas Nelson. Nelson Books and Thomas Nelson are registered trademarks of HarperCollins Christian Publishing, Inc.

Published in association with the A Group.

Thomas Nelson titles may be purchased in bulk for educational, business, fund-raising, or sales promotional use. For information, please e-mail SpecialMarkets@ThomasNelson.com.

In some instances, names, dates, locations, and other identifying details have been changed to protect the identities and privacy of those mentioned in this book.

Unless otherwise noted, Scripture quotations are taken from the Holy Bible, New International Version®, NIV®. Copyright © 1973, 1978, 1984, 2011 by Biblica, Inc.™ Used by permission of Zondervan. All rights reserved worldwide. www.zondervan.com

Scripture quotations marked ESV are from the ENGLISH STANDARD VERSION. © 2001 by Crossway Bibles, a division of Good News Publishers.

Scripture quotations marked HCSB are from the HOLMAN CHRISTIAN STANDARD BIBLE. © 1999, 2000, 2002, 2003 by Broadman and Holman Publishers. All rights reserved.

Scripture quotations marked KJV are from the King James Version.

Scripture quotations marked MSG are from *The Message* by Eugene H. Peterson. © 1993, 1994, 1995, 1996, 2000. Used by permission of NavPress Publishing Group. All rights reserved.

Scripture quotations marked NASB are from the NEW AMERICAN STANDARD BIBLE®, © The Lockman Foundation 1960, 1962, 1963, 1968, 1971, 1972, 1973, 1975, 1977, 1995. Used by permission.

Scripture quotations marked NKJV are from the NEW KING JAMES VERSION®. © 1982 by Thomas Nelson, Inc. Used by permission. All rights reserved.

Scripture quotations marked NLT are from *Holy Bible*, New Living Translation. © 1996, 2004, 2007. Used by permission of Tyndale House Publishers, Inc., Wheaton, Illinois 60189. All rights reserved.

ISBN: 978-0-5291-0270-6 (IE)

Library of Congress Cataloging-in-Publication Data

Catron, Jenni, 1976-
  Clout : discover and unleash your God-given influence / Jenni Catron.
    pages cm
  Includes bibliographical references.
  ISBN 978-1-4002-0568-4
1. Self-confidence--Religious aspects--Christianity. 2. Influence--Religious aspects--Christianity. I. Title.
  BV4598.23.C38 2014
  248.4--dc23

                    2013024274

Printed in the United States of America

16 17 18 RRD 6 5 4 3

To my husband, Merlyn, who always believes in me more than I believe in myself. Thank you for championing my dreams as if they were your own.

CONTENTS

Foreword   XV

Introduction: You Have "It"
    Understanding What Clout Is All About   xvii

PART ONE: THE 7 CLOUT KILLERS
    Chapter 1: You Don't Have to Be Afraid
    Confronting Fear   3

    Chapter 2: You More Than Measure Up
    Putting a Stop to Comparison   17

    Chapter 3: You Are Enough
    Understanding the Impact of Jealousy   31

    Chapter 4: You Have Enough
    Squeezing Out Scarcity   45

    Chapter 5: You Are Good Enough
    Identifying Insecurity   63

Chapter 6: You Don't Have to Know It All
Purging Pride 79

Chapter 7: You Can Let Go
Relinquishing Control 95

PART TWO: THE 4 CLOUT CULTIVATORS
Chapter 8: Discovering Your Identity 111

Chapter 9: Developing Your Confidence 127

Chapter 10: Defining Your Mission 139

Chapter 11: Determining Your Passion 153

Conclusion: Unleashing Your Clout 171

Acknowledgments 185

Resources 187

Notes 189

About the Author 199

FOREWORD

OKAY, I HAVE TO ADMIT THAT I DON'T READ MOST forewords because I figure the person writing it was asked to write it, did it as a favor, and felt compelled to help sell books and make the author look good. I suppose that's why I don't ask others to write forewords to my books, and why I decline many of the offers I get to write forewords for others, though I do feel bad for not accommodating them all.

I mention all this because this book, *Clout*, was given to me to read, and I immediately said, "Oh, I hope this author will let me write the foreword!" And there is only one reason for this—I think it is one of the best books I have ever read, and I want others to know about it.

I could tell you why I love the book, and I suppose that I will eventually do so in the next few paragraphs, but first I'll simply encourage you to flip through the book and read the italicized pull-quotes that are peppered throughout. If you're at all like me, you'll be convicted immediately. In a good way.

What Jenni Catron has done here is extract from flawed human nature the dangers that keep us from realizing the potential that God gives all of us. And she does so in a way that is at once frightening—really—and inspiring. As I was reading it I immediately wanted to scream, "Yes! This is what gets me into trouble!" And then I wanted to tell everyone else about it so they could make the same liberating realizations and get on with becoming the people they're meant to be.

Jenni has a wonderful way of highlighting the evidence of our brokenness—pride, jealousy, insecurity, scarcity, fear—without being at all condescending. She makes us want to become the best people we can be, the people we were created to be, and to help others do the same.

This book should be given to every high school student, college student, career-stalled employee, frustrated executive, and unfulfilled human being who deep down inside doesn't know what their mission in life is. I think that Jenni Catron has figured out what her mission in life is, and that *Clout* will be a classic for many years.

—Patrick Lencioni, president, The Table Group; best-selling author, *The Five Dysfunctions of a Team* and *The Advantage*

INTRODUCTION

You Have "It"

Understanding What Clout Is All About

NASHVILLE IS A CITY OF DREAMERS. IT'S ONE OF the things that I love about living here. Everyone is chasing a dream.

For the nine years that I worked in the music business I had a front-row seat to the dreamers. Some good. Some bad. But every once in a while we would stumble upon someone who just had "it"—the undeniable but immeasurable factor that just makes you say, "He was made to do this!" Each of those individuals is special. When they take the stage, they captivate you. You forget where you are and what you're doing, and you're mesmerized by watching them shine. You're fascinated by how powerfully yet effortlessly they display their talents.

It's not just the musicians either. When someone is exceptional at something, it impacts the world. Others take notice. It's the Peyton Mannings, Michael Jordans, and Roger Federers. It's the Steve Jobses, Donald Trumps, and Warren Buffetts. It's the Julia Robertses, Cary Grants, and Katharine Hepburns. It's the Mother Teresas, Eleanor Roosevelts, and William Wilberforces.

But you know what? It's also you and me. You have that "it" factor too. You were made to wield your God-given influence in such a way that makes others say, "She was made for that!" You have clout. The question is, have you discovered it yet?

Something deep inside each of us longs to count. We want to matter to the world. We long to make a difference. We get bored, tired, even depressed by routine and monotony. We're desperate for significance. We're searching for acknowledgment. We beam when someone says, "You matter." We seek praise, accolades, and awards, but somehow once we achieve them, they feel empty and we move on to another desperate search for the next fix that will affirm our worth.

We compete and compare. We boast and envy. We scrape and claw to amass as much as the next person and then become grossly annoyed with our lack of uniqueness and individuality.

Some people remain in this cycle of the insatiable quest for significance for decades, perhaps even their entire lives. They are convinced that something or someone will eventually fill this gaping hole of purpose.

Others more quickly recognize the futility of these efforts but are prone to wallow in the guilt and condemnation they associate with finding significance in trivial things. Recognizing the limited fulfillment of fleeting accomplishments, they begin to question their entire purpose.

We often try to ignore this aching hollowness or stuff it beneath the layers of fear, comparison, jealousy, scarcity, insecurity, pride, and control issues that gnaw at our souls. While we long for significance, we wrestle with whether that longing is good and godly. But what if it is? What if God expects us to discover and unleash our God-given influence—our *clout*?

Clout is the influence that God has given to you and to no one else. You are specifically designed to impact the world in a way that no one else can. Discovering your clout is an essential part of unleashing your purpose. You have a specific purpose, a calling, that only you are qualified to fulfill. Your God-given influence defines your purpose. Your purpose establishes your leadership. Your leadership makes a mark on the world.

You have a specific purpose, a calling, that only you are qualified to fulfill.

In order to understand what clout is and how to operate from it, we need to do some work to unpack false assumptions and perceptions. We assume we don't have what it takes. We perceive we don't measure up. We believe we are not enough. These are some enemies of our influence that can hold us back, trip us up, and keep us from fully unleashing our influence and living our purpose. Let's call them clout killers. They're the villains that set out to derail us before we've even fully begun to discover what our God-given influence looks like.

How do I know? I have been there. I have lived it. For the majority of my life I found my purpose and identity in fleeting accomplishments and empty acknowledgments. And then one beautifully normal day all my dreams came screeching to a halt. My career, upon which I had built all my self-worth, crumbled. I had no control over its unraveling, and I had no idea who I was without it.

That crisis of purpose forced me to recognize that over the course of my life, I had learned to listen to myriad voices telling me what to do and who to be. They were the voices of fear, comparison, jealousy, scarcity, insecurity, pride, and control. Those voices were shaping me but not in the way that I hoped. They were killing my influence rather than developing it. They were holding me back rather than propelling me forward. My quest for influence was not established upon the foundation of God's perspective on my influence and leadership. It was precariously teetering on the misguided information from natural but inherently lethal enemies of my influence. In all my attempts to discover God's purpose for my life and leadership, I had started the search without a compass.

That season of my life forced me to recognize the shaky foundation upon which I had built all my dreams. My dreams, goals, and plans were based on my false assumptions about myself, others, and God. I believed if I intended to make a difference with my life, it was up to me to figure out how. I quickly learned that if I worked a little harder and a little longer than everyone else, I would stand out. I didn't really believe God was all that interested in my daily decisions. I didn't believe anyone else cared. If I was going to succeed, I had to make it happen. And worst of all, I believed I could do it all—until the day arrived that I couldn't.

I had unknowingly been driven by forces that lulled me to believe I had power that I never had. I had become numb to my feelings of fear, insecurity, and jealousy, and I was ignoring my tendency to compare, act out of scarcity, be prideful, and control. These clout killers were manipulating me into believing I had greater influence than I actually had. When my career—the idol I had allowed to define my purpose—was upended by a corporate merger and sizable restructuring, the shaky foundation of my influence was revealed.

What I've learned after years of sharing my story and hearing so many of yours is that we all do this in one way or another. We find a faulty foundation upon which we establish our sense of purpose.

I believe it's essential that you recognize as soon as possible how you've shaped your view of yourself. Everything you do springs from this perception. Your clout is your God-given influence. How you manage it determines your leadership impact.

Author and leadership expert John Maxwell is famously quoted for saying, "Leadership is influence—nothing more, nothing less."[1] For years I didn't agree with him. I believed that leadership was so much more. *Influence* didn't seem to be a big enough or a demanding enough word to describe it. But perhaps I was wrestling with that simple definition because my understanding of influence was skewed. I hadn't yet grasped the depth of what influence really is. When we discover and unleash our God-given influence, we position ourselves to lead with passion and purpose that defy our personal limitations. That's what clout is all about.

> *When we discover and unleash our God-given influence, we position ourselves to lead with passion and purpose that defy our personal limitations.*

Discovering and unleashing my God-given influence began with this passage from Galatians: *"Make a careful exploration of who you are and the work you have been given, and then sink yourself into that. Don't be impressed with yourself. Don't compare yourself with others. Each of you must take responsibility for doing the creative best you can with your own life"* (6:4–5 MSG).

Clout is a funny thing. It's polarizing. We spend enormous amounts of time chasing it only to wrestle with another range of emotions when we have it. Some of us will be terrified of our influence. Others will become prideful and arrogant. Some of us will deny we have it, while others will eagerly flaunt it.

Clout looks different for each of us. A world leader may influence millions while a stay-at-home mom may influence just a few. No matter how large the arena of influence, however, the impact to each individual is equally significant.

We must develop clout to make an impact. Undeveloped influence leaves others wanting and perhaps even neglected. When we mismanage our influence on someone else's life, we may affect the trajectory of that person's influence. Misdirected influence can wreak havoc on its victims. Unexplored influence leaves us leading aimless or distracted lives where our deepest dreams and longings remain uncultivated.

Influence doesn't ensure notoriety or popularity. It doesn't necessarily mean a career change or a major life-altering event. Unleashing your God-given influence means leading your life from a place of deep purpose and confidence. It's taking what you've been given and using it to do the remarkable. It's recognizing that little in life happens by accident, but you can use everything in life for a purpose that is greater than yourself. Influence is recognizing that you are making a mark on others whether or not you're trying to do that. Influence is understanding that what you do today matters, so give it everything you've got.

Clout is a journey to leading from your God-given influence. Whether you lead yourself, your family, or a Fortune 500 company, a healthy understanding of who you are is the starting point for courageous leadership. It's a journey to pursue the confidence that is found in a well-defined purpose. In part 1 we'll confront the clout killers that challenge us: fear, comparison, jealousy, scarcity, insecurity, pride, and control, and we'll identify the replacements that allow us to take responsibility for doing the creative best we can with our lives. In part 2 we'll create a new framework for discovering our God-given influence and building a solid foundation from which our leadership can thrive.

I'm more convinced than ever that God gives us big dreams. It's how we direct those dreams that makes all the difference.

Clout will give you the courage to step confidently into your God-given sphere of influence.

PART 1

THE 7 CLOUT KILLERS

Fear
Comparison
Jealousy
Scarcity
Insecurity
Pride
Control

CHAPTER 1

YOU DON'T HAVE TO BE AFRAID

Confronting Fear

Courage is resistance to fear, mastery of fear, not absence of fear.

—MARK TWAIN[1]

BRIAN IS AN INCREDIBLY SMART, STRONG, AND confident individual. With a decade of tenure at his company, a robust staff, and the experience and knowledge to substantiate his value to the organization, Brian seemingly had nothing to fear. He was next in line for the executive suite. On the outside looking in, you would assume that Brian was completely confident. He knew how to create a polished exterior that projected self-assurance. Brian and I worked down the hall from each other. It never occurred to me to ask him if he ever wrestled with

3

fear until the day he was handed the pink slip and ushered out the door. In a struggling economy, the company he was loyal to couldn't be loyal to him.

Over lunch a few weeks later, I probed a bit: "Did you see this coming?" His response was casual but measured: "I always feared it could happen. Not because I wasn't performing but because I've always lived with a fear that I'm not enough. I've always had an underlying fear that someday I wouldn't be enough. I would make one too many mistakes. I'd miss an important detail. But I didn't expect to be dismissed this way. It makes me question, why wasn't I valuable enough to keep?"

Brian's fears and questions are significant. They represent an underlying tension that challenges our clout every day. *Am I enough?*

The question is overwhelming because of the numerous fears that underlie it. Our fears are so diverse and so extreme that we're more apt to avoid and ignore them rather than acknowledge that they're there.

In her best-selling book *Feel the Fear . . . and Do It Anyway*, Susan Jeffers places fear into three categories. Level 1 fears are those that happen to us (aging or being in an accident) as well as those that require actions from us (changing careers or public speaking).[2] "Level 2 fears have to do with *inner states of mind* rather than exterior situations" (fear of being rejected or fear of being vulnerable).[3] Level 3 fear is "the biggest fear of all—the one that really keeps you stuck." It is the fear that "I can't handle it!"[4] Jeffers writes, "At the bottom of every one of your fears is simply the fear that you can't handle whatever life may bring you."[5] Or said another way, it's the fear that "I am not enough."

Fear is the front-runner of the clout killers. As we begin to unpack these inhibitors to our confidence and influence, we'll see a consistent theme of fear. Fear tends to coerce its tentacles into all our issues. We fear that who we are is not enough, so we deal with jealousy. We fear not having enough, so we live out of scarcity. We fear not being good enough, so we live with insecurity. We fear not being strong enough, so we cover it up with pride. We fear not measuring up to others, so we wrestle with comparison. We fear chaos, so we grapple for control. This fear that we can't handle it, that we're not enough, rings true in each of these enemies that impact our influence. What we'll discover is that our greatest fear is true, but there is an even greater truth to replace it.

Do Not Be Afraid

You don't have to be afraid. Easier said than done, right? Again and again in the Bible God told his children not to be afraid. Through a vision, God said,

> *Do not be afraid, Abram.*
> *I am your shield,*
> *your very great reward. (Gen. 15:1)*

When Hagar and her son Ishmael were banished from Abraham's land, an angel told Hagar, "Do not be afraid; God has heard" (Gen. 21:17). When Isaac was expelled from his land by the Philistines and forced to move from place to place, God appeared to him and reminded him, "Do not be afraid, for I am with you" (Gen. 26:24). When Jacob was fearful of traveling in his old age, God told him, "Do not be afraid to go down to Egypt, for I will make you into a great nation" (Gen. 46:3). Numerous times Moses reminded the Israelites not to be afraid because God was with them and would fight for them. And after Moses' death, God made the same commitment to Joshua as he encouraged him to be strong and courageous: "Do not be afraid; do not be discouraged, for the LORD your God will be with you wherever you go" (Josh. 1:9).

From David to Elijah, from Isaiah to Jeremiah, God continuously reminded his people not to fear. When Joseph considered canceling his engagement to Mary, an angel appeared to him, telling him not to be afraid (Matt. 1:19–20). When Jesus charged the twelve disciples with their responsibility, he told them not to be afraid of those who would seek to harm them for proclaiming the truth (Matt. 10:26–28). From the women gathering at the empty tomb to the disciples seeing the resurrected Jesus, the message was the same: do not be afraid (Matt. 28:5, 10).

In every instance, people faced legitimate fears. But each time God's message remained consistent. It seems God understood that we would wrestle with fear.

FEAR IMPACTS OUR INFLUENCE

September 11, 2001, was a chilling day for the people of the United States. But for the mayor of New York City, Rudy Giuliani, it was a day that distinctly impacted the trajectory of his leadership influence. For a city facing the most devastating tragedy our country has known, the mayor was at a crossroads of influence. How he handled that moment would redefine his leadership.

Everything he had achieved to that point, every ounce of influence he had earned, had prepared him for that moment. Facing his fears quickly was essential to helping lead others through theirs.

May 1, 2010, was the day of my crossroads of influence. As the rain continued to fall and riverbanks overflowed, there was an eerie moment of awareness when I realized the situation was serious. Our great city was flooding, and we had to step up to help. Although inhibited by sporadic cell phone service and the inability to gather in one place, our lead pastor, a few of our staff, and I began to plan how Cross Point Church could help. We knew it was our moment to rise up and provide support and hope to a terrified city.

We often confront our greatest fear at the crossroads of influence. We face our greatest fear at the threshold of our greatest opportunity to make an impact. Not to confront this fear would be to deny who we are created to be. We'd be sabotaging the very calling and purpose we are designed for.

We often confront our greatest fear at the crossroads of influence.

Fear finds us at the edge of the cliff: the moment when we must make a decision. When you find yourself there, do you give in to fear or step out in faith? Fear turns tail and runs. Faith takes the leap. Faith sees beyond the fear and recognizes that you were uniquely designed and created for this moment.

God equips us with plans to use us. Yet I believe that many of us miss opportunities to cultivate our influence because we choose the wrong route at the crossroads of influence. We turn around and run back when faith requires a leap that we're too afraid to take.

One thing that I love about my job is that I have the privilege of helping develop other leaders. I love seeing young leaders grow. But every once in a while they will hit a growth hurdle that they can't overcome. Rarely do they lack the ability. Most often the growth challenge in front of them forces them to confront a fear that they are unwilling to face. Their unwillingness to confront that fear causes them to shrink back or to cover it up. Their attempts to avoid the issue ultimately lead to an erosion of trust with the people they influence.

Alex had the makings of a star staff member. He was passionate about his job. He had inspired vision for where he wanted to lead people. He was eager to step in and provide leadership to a group that had been floundering for some time. As his leader, I was so excited for him and the possibilities of growth ahead. The first year was challenging, but he kept his chin up and pushed through difficult growing pains. But soon I began to notice signs of discouragement in his eyes. Something had changed, but I couldn't pinpoint it. I saw fear instead of excitement and optimism. Where I still saw obvious potential, he saw roadblocks.

Over the next six months the situation deteriorated. I couldn't make sense of why things were spiraling south so quickly. Gradually as I kept engaging him in conversation, he shared that he was terrified of being a failure. He feared that he wasn't capable of doing the job that he had been hired to do. His fear that others would see him as a failure caused him to try to cover it up rather than share that he was struggling. Because he wouldn't confront the fear with truth, many of those he influenced eventually lost trust in him.

FEAR HIDES

Elizabeth was the victim of childhood sexual abuse. She didn't feel safe and secure in her home; she lived with the daily fear of being victimized. She also lived with the fear of what would happen if anyone found out. Worse yet, she was threatened that if she told others, they wouldn't believe her, and she would suffer the consequences. Elizabeth's fragile young heart couldn't discern the lie within those threats. Because she was terrified of telling anyone about the abuse, those who were best able to help her were kept in the dark and unable to clarify the truth for her.

It's fairly common for children to hide out of fear, but if we carry that tendency into adulthood, we will live in the darkness of untruth. As adults we often try to hide from our fear by ignoring that it's there. Rather than acknowledge it and replace it with truth, we allow ourselves to live with the darkness it creates. We don't want to acknowledge we fear failure, so we cover it up with pride and the drive to perform.

FEAR ISOLATES

During a particularly challenging and stressful season of work, I was wrestling with deep insecurities. Afraid that I wasn't cut out for the level of leadership I held, my mind began spinning off multiple worst-case scenarios, pricking all my greatest fears—fear of failing, fear of being fired, fear of not leading well, fear of making poor decisions, on and on it went. As I lay in bed one night unable to sleep because of the speed at which my mind was racing, I shared my thoughts and feelings with my husband. He was shocked by the emotional load I was carrying.

I was amazed at how freeing it was to verbalize my fears. I didn't realize how lonely and isolated I was by wallowing in those fears by myself. Giving voice to them allowed me to share the burden, and more important, my husband had the opportunity to speak truth to the isolation that fear dangerously creates.

In the isolation of our minds, fear can be tormenting. The truth found in 2 Timothy 1:7 is an important reminder: "God has not given us a spirit of fear, but of power and of love and of a sound mind" (NKJV).

We fear not having enough, so we are scarce with praise and stingy with our resources, which continues to close us off from developing relationships with others.

We fear that others won't love or accept us for who we are. Our imperfections feed our insecurity, so we remain distanced and walled off from others.

When we verbalize fear, it loses its power. Sharing our fear with someone else lessens its power over us.

Fear Paralyzes

Fear can also paralyze us from moving forward. We fear chaos, so our constant need for control causes us to slow things down while we try to get a handle on it. Our need for control can become paralyzing and is extraordinarily dangerous to our leadership and influence. If we're unable to get some sense of control, we may give up altogether.

I have observed this tendency play out with some of the best leaders. Every leader at one time or another gets to a point of feeling paralyzed. If leaders are not coached through it, they will stall—if not kill—their influence and miss their opportunity to live out their God-given influence.

Economist and political adviser John Kenneth Galbraith once said, "All of the great leaders have had one characteristic in common: it was the willingness to confront unequivocally the major anxiety of their people in their time."[6] To influence others you have to help move them to new realities and possibilities. You can't take them where you haven't led yourself. You must be willing to confront your fears and lead others through theirs.

> *You must be willing to confront your fears and lead others through theirs.*

EXCHANGING FEAR FOR TRUTH

We know how fear affects us. We acknowledge the darkness, isolation, and inactivity that accompany it, but how do we overcome it? We read all the "do not be afraid" scriptures and are more likely to feel guilt for not having the faith to overcome it than find peace in those statements.

But take another look at every time God says, "Do not be afraid." Notice that his message doesn't end there. Behind every statement he gives us a reason why we shouldn't fear. "Do not be afraid" technically should be enough because he is God. But he knew that our fears need to be replaced with strong promises. We need to replace fear with truth. Consider the statements of truth that followed "do not be afraid . . ."

I am your shield, / your very great reward. (Gen. 15:1)
God has heard. (Gen. 21:17)
for I am with you. (Isa. 41:10)

for the Lord your God will be with you wherever you go.
   (Josh 1:9)
you have found favor with God. (Luke 1:30)

We must confront our fears with the truth, and that truth is the powerful reminder of God's constant presence. Sarah Young wrote of Jesus' instruction in her devotional *Jesus Calling:* "When you view events from this perspective—through the Light of My universal Presence—fear loses its grip on you."[7]

Our core fear that we can't handle it, that we're not enough, I believe it. I don't think we can handle it, at least not on our own. We're not expected to handle it on our own. Notice that in all the examples in Scripture, God doesn't say, "Do not be afraid. You've got this!" He says, "Do not be afraid. I've got this." That basic truth has the power to overcome all our fears if we allow it to.

Philippians 4:13 is such a familiar reminder that we almost miss it: "I can do all things through Christ who strengthens me" (NKJV). Our ability is in his strength. God's constant presence is the greater truth that confronts our ultimate fear.

When we ignore God's presence in the fear equation, we lead from a place of vulnerability. Every time we make a fear-based decision we lose a bit more influence. It borders on irresponsibility if we're not careful. When we lead from fear, we make reactionary decisions. Those we lead can sense our fear and are influenced by it. Our fear-based decisions erode our influence rather than provide strength for others and instill their confidence in us as a result of our sound leadership.

> *Every time we make a fear-based decision we lose a bit more influence.*

Lynne Hybels, wife of Willow Creek Community Church's senior pastor, described how fear affects our influence: "Fear magnifies our weaknesses and it hides our potential."[8] Ironically all the weaknesses we're trying to cover up are magnified when we allow fear to overtake us. Worse yet, our potential—our careful exploration of who we are and the work we've been given—gets buried under that fear. Instead of seeing the truth of the confident child of God who knows his or her calling and purpose, others see a fearful, insecure, controlling wannabe leader frantically making reactionary decisions.

CONFRONTING FEAR

Remember Brian from the beginning of the chapter? Brian's fear of not being enough was seemingly validated by his being let go from his job. Had he allowed that fear to continue to fuel him, the trajectory of his influence could have taken a turn for worse. But instead, Brian chose to focus on what was true. He was educated. He had great experience.

While he was a casualty of corporate downsizing, his unemployment was not an indicator of his clout. He had God-given influence that needed a new environment in which to thrive. With these truths in mind he reached out to family, friends, and mentors who could affirm him and give him good counsel. He chose to immediately network and look for other opportunities. By replacing his fear with truth, Brian chose a path that allowed his God-given influence to be even further defined. By confronting his fear, he began to redefine how he could best live out his clout.

What is the fear that you're facing? Are you keeping it in the dark? Is it isolating you? How is it paralyzing you? Where is it affecting your influence? What is the truth that you need to apply to your fear to help you overcome it?

I grew up in a small town in the Midwest. I was blessed with family who loved me and a safe, secure community. It was comfortable. But comfort can insulate us from facing our fears. When I chose to move away and pursue a different career path than the paths of my family and friends, my fears ranged from the practical *(How am I going to pay for this? Where am I going to live?)* to the psychological *(Am I cut out for this? What if I fail?)*. I had convinced myself that if I faced these fears this one time, I would never face them again. I believed that my fears were just one hurdle. After I leaped over it effectively, I would be home free the rest of the race.

But fears are like an ongoing series of hurdles. Once we take one of them, we'll have only a minute to catch our breath before we tackle the next one. We need to recognize and acknowledge that fear will never go away. As long as we're continuing to grow and expand our influence, we will be confronted with new fears. That's growth. That's progress. I believe that God allows us to be confronted repeatedly with fear in order to remind us of the power of truth. Every hurdle of fear is an opportunity for our faith to grow.

> *Every hurdle of fear is an opportunity for our faith to grow.*

Facing our fear doesn't mean ignoring it, hiding it, or avoiding it. Facing our fear doesn't mean trying to control the fear away. Facing our fear means acknowledging our fear and going ahead anyway. Parker J. Palmer stated, "'Be not afraid' does not mean we cannot *have* fear. Everyone has fear, and people who embrace the call to leadership often find fear abounding. Instead, the words say we do not need to *be* the fear we have. We do not have to lead from a place of fear, thereby engendering a world in which fear is multiplied."[9] We need to move forward despite our fear because we are equipped with the truth to confront it.

There is a significant distinction between caution and fear in the context of this discussion. A caution suggests imminent danger. We have caution when we face a threat to our safety or consider reckless or sinful behavior. Caution gives reason to pause and consider the truth. When caution is confronted by truth, it often changes the course of our action. The fear I'm describing is the fear that holds us back or hinders us from moving forward because of the unknown. The fear that "I can't handle it" when confronted with truth always propels us toward becoming a truer picture of who we are designed to be.

The next several chapters will challenge you to face the fears that impact your influence—fear of not measuring up, fear of not being enough, fear of not having enough, fear of not being good enough, fear of weakness, and fear of losing control. These are the clout killers, the fears that repeatedly hinder you. If you don't address these issues now, they may disqualify you at the crossroads of influence.

In his book *Fearless*, Max Lucado defined *truth* this way: "When Christ is great, our fears are not."[10] Your God-given influence emerges when you confidently begin to confront your fears and replace them with truth.

DISCOVERY STEPS

- What fears make you feel that you can't handle it? Take a few minutes and write them down.
- What truth from Scripture confronts that fear?
- Review the promises that God made to his people in Scripture when they were afraid. Which one of these promises do you need to remember?

CHAPTER 2

YOU MORE THAN MEASURE UP

Putting a Stop to Comparison

*Now much time and leisure doth he gain, who is not
curious to know what his neighbour hath said, or hath
done, or hath attempted, but only what he doth himself,
that it may be just and holy?*

—Marcus Aurelius[1]

IN 2005 I TOOK THE LEAP FROM A THRIVING
career in the music business to become executive director of
Cross Point Church. As a founding member of Cross Point, I
was overly confident in my ability to step into this role, assuming that I had a pretty good understanding of the culture and the
expectations. I wasn't prepared for how challenging it would be
for my personality to flourish in our ministry context. While I

am a very strong, driven, type A leader, I am also very much an introvert. I have learned appropriate social skills and professionalism to be "on" when the leadership role calls for it.

I am quite content and feel inspired, however, when I can power through a project in the quiet of my office. Time and time again I had received feedback, sometimes given with love and sincere concern and other times with criticism, that I was not being as social as my ministry counterparts. With a genuine desire to grow and a determination to measure up to my peers, I attempted to stretch myself into more extroverted situations. I committed to dinners and events that I typically would not be interested in, I worked the room instead of enjoying the comfortable conversation of a select few, and I put off important projects in an effort to be more available.

After several years of this constant striving to measure up to my more extroverted comrades, I was on the brink of burnout. I was exhausted, miserable, and desperate for something to change. I felt completely inadequate, unaccepted, and incompetent. What's worse is that my effectiveness as a leader was waning because I was so drained from trying to be someone other than myself. I had convinced myself that the most successful leaders were more gregarious and charming. I envied the ease with which they were everything I was not. And I resented the fact that as much as I tried, I could not be like them. Comparison was robbing me of the confidence that comes from leading from my God-given influence.

Comparison is a clever clout killer because at a surface level it doesn't look all that dangerous. It's the fuel that propels us forward. It's often the motivation to do greater things. Comparison in our culture is natural, perhaps even expected.

Everything about us is measured from the day we are born. Our birth announcements proudly declare our height and weight. Our routine pediatric appointments measure our growth percentiles, our athletic ability is gauged against our peers', and our academic prowess is measured by quarterly report cards. And it doesn't end there. SAT scores, college entrance exams, salaries, job titles, neighborhoods, social status, and family dynamics—it's all weighed and measured. Our American culture begs us to compare and conform from the time we are born.

Comparison triggers the fear that "I don't measure up; I am not enough." The fear of not measuring up robs us of seeing the value in our influence, and it keeps us on a perpetual quest to be better than others. Comparison berates us with questions: *Did I speak as dynamically as he did? Did I lead through a challenge as effectively as she would? Did I encourage and celebrate my coworkers or staff as well as another? Did I prepare the report as thoroughly? Did I outperform my greatest rival on this month's sales goal? Did I parent as effectively as my friend? Did I plan the most unique birthday party for my child? Did I hit the longest drive of the match?*

In the middle of the passage about understanding our God-given influence, we're blasted with a strong and direct statement: "Don't compare yourself with others" (Gal. 6:4–5 MSG). The first time I read this it felt too abrupt. I wanted it to say more. I needed it to be coupled with disclaimers. As I processed it, I was forced to realize that for most of my life I thought comparison was the way to navigate the world—see what others are doing, compare that to my life, make adjustments, and compare again. I believed that comparison was a necessary skill for survival in a world that compares and competes over everything.

The problem with comparison is that it doesn't end with a simple sizing up. It's humanly impossible to compare oneself to what someone else has accomplished and not be tempted by the sins of envy, jealousy, and greed. The Bible calls comparison the sin of covetousness (Luke 12:15). It lures us to deeply desire what another person has, including God-given influence, gifts, talents, experiences, and opportunities, all the while discrediting our own. We essentially reject how God has uniquely created and gifted us and covet what he's given to others.

Our temptation to compare distracts us from being who God has called us to be.

Our temptation to compare distracts us from being who God has called us to be. Rather than focus on what God has purposefully designed us for, we distract ourselves with this clout killer that robs us of leading from a place of security and confidence.

COMPARISON IMPACTS OUR INFLUENCE

Because we're so busy comparing, we can miss the damage that comparison inflicts on our influence. Comparison impacts us and our relationships in significant ways. Let's consider a few:

COMPARISON DISTORTS OUR VIEW OF OURSELVES

Comparison twists what should be unique about us into something that we are either grossly dissatisfied with or disproportionately proud of. Pastor Robert Morris, of Gateway Church in Texas, says, "When you compare yourself to someone you're either going to feel inferior or superior."[2] While comparison fixates us on what we don't have and how we don't measure up, comparison also takes us to the other extreme where we begin to see ourselves as better than others. We pridefully position ourselves above others. Even the disciples were guilty of asking Jesus who was greatest among them (Luke 9:46–48). The pendulum swing of comparison has us envying one person and diminishing the value of another.

COMPARISON LEADS TO OTHER SINS

When we compare, the inconsistencies in how we measure up begin to lead us down the trail to other sins. If we feel less than someone else, we are liable to wrestle with envy, jealousy, and insecurity. If we stack up stronger than another, we are likely to be tempted by greed, selfishness, and pride.

Furthermore we may blame God and allow anger, resentment, and ingratitude to take root. Pastor Morris goes on to say, "Comparison produces anger and resentment towards God. Covetousness is greed and selfishness with a mask. Covetousness is ingratitude at the highest level with a fist in the face of God."[3]

COMPARISON ROBS US OF OUR INDIVIDUALITY

When I worked in the music business, I often had the privilege of scouting new talent. Our A&R (Artists and Repertoire) team hosted showcases for new artists to perform for our staff. More often than not, the new bands sounded like established, highly successful acts. These young bands aspired to the success of a band they admired and attempted to mimic it rather than create their own sound. We were so disappointed because we were desperate to hear their uniqueness. They were desperate to fit in. As a result, both sides of the business missed out on their potential.

Paul used the analogy of the human body to explain the value of each person's unique contribution and noted, "God has put the body together . . . so that there should be no division in the body, but that its parts should have equal concern for each other" (1 Cor. 12:24–25). He didn't say that we have equal gifts or equal responsibilities; instead we're to have "equal concern for each other." While our roles, responsibilities, and visibility may be different, we're instructed to treat each other with equal care or importance. Another version *(The Message)* of this passage says that we're to be dependent on each other. If our comparison leads to anything, it should lead to care for each other. And what's more significant is that it's all for the purpose of unity rather than division.

COMPARISON DISTRACTS, DEMOTIVATES, AND DISCOURAGES US

Comparison slows us down and takes our focus off the influence we're trying to unleash. We lose the will to continue because we feel that we're never measuring up. When comparing ourselves to others is the measurement we live by, we're constantly positioned for failure.

Jeff Henderson, the lead pastor of Gwinnett Church in the Atlanta area, is one of the most gifted leaders I know, and he has been an incredible mentor to me. He expressed his concern about comparison:

There's far too much time and energy wasted on studying the competition. We will never find our true potential by comparing ourselves to others. Only by comparing ourselves and our organizations to our own potential will we find unchartered territories and possibilities.

The people and organizations you respect the most do just that. You can too. Stop comparing yourself to others. Start comparing yourself to your own God-given potential. This is where true uniqueness and creativity is found.[4]

COMPARISON ERODES TEAM UNITY

I work with a pretty amazing group of people. For the most part I would say that our team does a great job celebrating each other, but every once in a while comparison creeps in. I hear comments that suggest some roles are considered more significant than others. This shows up consistently between more public roles and behind-the-scenes administrative roles. One cannot exist without the other, but too often, in any organization, the more prominent leadership roles are more highly favored while support staff roles are diminished. Successful teams identify ways to make sure that all team members are celebrated and valued for their contributions.

As leaders, we can be guilty of comparing employees. Our natural inclination is to compare an employee's performance to how we would have performed the task or to how another employee has done it. Often without realizing it we create a competitive environment for our employees by how we measure their performance. Your clout as a leader strategically positions you to help bring out the unique gifts and contributions of each staff member. Be mindful of the temptation to compare one's performance to another and expect unnecessary uniformity. Your organization will benefit from each person's applying a unique perspective or skill.

God is calling us to value each other for our differences. Understanding this is foundational to understanding our clout. Our influence is most significant when we quit attempting to mimic someone else. When we embrace our influence and champion the influence of others, we begin to see the power of our distinctiveness coming together as a unified force.

CONFRONTING COMPARISON

W. Chan Kim and Renée Mauborgne wrote the business book *Blue Ocean Strategy*. Their appeal was that an organization should create new demand in an "uncontested market space," or a blue ocean, rather than compete head-to-head with other suppliers in an existing industry.[5] Observing how companies were competing like sharks in a bloody ocean for the same consumers and market share, Kim and Mauborgne believed that companies could find their blue ocean and create a new market. *Blue Ocean Strategy* changed the paradigm for business leaders and, with thorough research and strong argument, made a case for businesses understanding and identifying what they could uniquely do differently rather than comparing themselves to the competition and doing what everyone else is doing. You could say, Kim and Mauborgne were challenging businesses to better understand their clout.

We, too, must find our blue oceans. We must quit competing and comparing with others and start identifying what our God-given influence looks like. When we compare we squander our God-given influence. We miss our potential and the opportunities or possibilities that we could be charting.

I often wonder how much more God could use our influence if we weren't so preoccupied comparing ourselves to everyone else. What if we quit trying to fit in and fully embraced our differences as gifts given to us to radically impact the world? What if putting an end to comparison was the beginning of leading from

> *When we compare we squander our God-given influence. We miss our potential and the opportunities or possibilities that we could be charting.*

our God-given influence? We should be comparing ourselves only to our God-given potential. How can you begin to measure your influence against the gifts, talents, experiences, and opportunities that God has given you rather than against what he's given others? This is how you begin to define your clout.

EXCHANGING COMPARISON FOR FOCUS

From the age of thirteen I had dreamed of being a record company executive. I chose the college I attended based on its proximity to Nashville, where I intended to make my home. I diligently studied the record company where I planned to work, and once I landed an internship there, I worked feverishly to prove that I was employee material. Nearly nine years of hard work and purposeful ladder climbing positioned me just seats away from the desk I hoped to occupy one day. Every step of that journey was a constant game of comparison. As long as I edged out my peers just a bit, I felt secure in my ascent.

And then seemingly out of nowhere a series of circumstances caused me to question the entire trajectory I had planned. I thought I understood what my leadership needed to look like. I thought I understood my sphere of influence to be forever the world of music. When that plan was called into question, I was left with nothing to use for comparison. There was nothing for me to measure my worth or progress against. I had to become singularly focused on understanding what God wanted to do with my life and influence. Stripped of obvious comparisons, I was forced to focus on discovering and unleashing my God-given influence.

The replacement for comparison isn't overly profound. In fact, it's simple: Focus on the work you've been given. Take the focus off what you don't have, and more fully develop your God-given influence. Romans 12:3 reminds us: "Do not think of yourself more highly than you ought, but rather think of yourself with sober judgment." Since comparison can be fueled by self-centeredness, we might be tempted to think this verse tells us not to think about ourselves at all. It actually says not to think *more highly* of yourself than you should, but use sober judgment. Having sober judgment means having a realistic assessment of your gifts, or as Galatians 6:4 explains it: "Make a careful exploration of who you are and the work you have been given" (MSG).

In the spring of 2013, Cross Point partnered with several churches around the country for the END IT Movement, an initiative to bring awareness to the gravity of human slavery in the world. In our Sunday services we shared statistics as well as stories of others who are stepping up to bring awareness to the issue. One person we interviewed was singer-songwriter Natalie Grant. Burdened by the fact that there are twenty-seven million slaves in our world today, Natalie started an organization called Abolition International to provide hope and freedom to victims.

Natalie recognizes that her God-given influence as an award-winning recording artist has given her a platform from which she can share the need and enlist others to get involved. Although Natalie's story is incredibly inspiring, I was equally impressed by the phone call I received the next morning from another young woman who had attended the service that weekend.

Susan went home Sunday afternoon burdened by the stories that she had heard but unsure about what she could do to make a difference. She didn't feel called to start an organization or even to volunteer at a local agency. And then it dawned on her. As a local news reporter she could take her platform and help bring awareness to the issue. A pitch to her superiors and a few phone calls later, one of the major news outlets was covering the story. She had done her part. She had taken her God-given influence and made a difference. While at first Susan was tempted to compare herself to Natalie, she quickly turned her focus toward what she could do with the sphere of influence that God had given her.

When we can find peace with the gifts that we've been given and aren't tempted to compare ourselves with others at every turn, we begin to enjoy the freedom and purpose of living from our unique God-given influence.

Paul encouraged believers: "Let the one who boasts boast in the Lord" (2 Cor. 10:17). He reminded us to focus on our lives and calling and not be tempted to compare ourselves to others. When we're focused on God's will and plan for us, we don't have time to be distracted by how those things compare or measure up to others. The clout God intends for us to live out is always greater than we would have planned for ourselves. When we embrace the sphere of influence he has designed for us, we don't have time to think about anything else, let alone get bogged down in comparing our paths to that of anyone else.

Replacing comparison in our lives begins with making a concerted effort to focus on discovering and unleashing our God-given influence. Comparison holds us back and distracts us from this purpose. It keeps our focus on what we *don't* have rather than on what we *do* have.

During numerous seasons in my life I've been tempted by comparison. I've compared myself to friends, coworkers, family members, celebrities—anyone I perceived to have a better life than mine, anyone who had something that I longed for. In an attempt to replace my destructive thought patterns, I created a "what's good" list every morning. It was usually no more than three to five things that were good in my life at that point, such as a project that I completed at work, a friendship that was thriving, and an opportunity that I was pursuing. This exercise allowed me to focus on what was happening in my life and where God was using my gifts and influence for good. And it kept me from unnecessarily focusing on what others were doing. It was a daily reminder of the clout that God had given me and the ways that it could flourish if I chose to focus on it rather than on others.

> *The clout God intends for us to live out is always greater than we would have planned for ourselves.*

In its wildly popular StrengthsFinder assessment, the Gallup organization describes people strong in "Focus" as those who "can take a direction, follow through, and make the corrections necessary to stay on track. They prioritize, then act."[6]

Focusing on our God-given influence overrides our temptation to compare. If we are laser-focused on understanding how

God has equipped us, we will be less likely to be distracted by seeing how we measure up to others.

Overcoming the urge to make comparisons isn't a one-time battle, however. It will creep up time and time again. New relationships and new experiences will trigger those dormant roots, and you'll wrestle with it. But each time comparison attempts to spring up, you have a choice to replace it by focusing on what's good about what God is doing in you.

DISCOVERY STEPS

- For one day write down every time you are tempted to compare yourself to others. Keep a detailed journal of the people you compare yourself to and why.
- What sins does comparison usually lead to in your life: envy, jealousy, insecurity, greed, selfishness, pride, anger, resentment, or ingratitude?
- In all your comparisons, what are you missing about your unique God-given influence?

CHAPTER 3

YOU ARE ENOUGH

Understanding the Impact of Jealousy

Just as iron is eaten away by rust, so are the envious consumed by their envy.

—ANTISTHENES[1]

OUR ENTIRE STAFF WAS EAGER FOR JEFF TO arrive. We were shocked that he was leaving his prestigious company to join our small and scrappy team. I was feeling pretty proud of myself that we were able to woo him our way. The first few weeks were fabulous, but little by little I noticed that he was getting more time with the boss than I was. His ideas were being championed more. He was going on special trips and being invited to important meetings. I had lost the luster as the favored one, and I was not content to stand by and remain in that position.

What followed wasn't pretty. Jealous of the attention and favor I perceived I was losing, I looked for faults in Jeff. My well-developed root of jealousy found subtle ways to point out his weaknesses to others. My *concerns* about him were really nasty barbs covered with false compassion. In an effort to protect and defend my territory, I allowed jealousy to drive me to build a case against Jeff, but my jealous behavior only diminished my credibility. No one wants to listen to jealous ramblings. I was losing the influence I was so desperately trying to keep.

Jealousy is the irrational fear of losing something or someone valuable to you—with an emphasis on losing *to someone else*. We all fear losing things sacred to us, especially those we love, but that fear turns to jealousy because of the key phrase "to someone else." Our fears become irrationally jealous when we fixate on the person to whom we could lose.

The most valuable thing that we as leaders stand to lose is our clout. Jealousy sabotages our influence when we fear losing our influence to another person who shares our arena. It could be the coworker who is getting more of the boss's attention. It could be the new committee member whose ideas are constantly celebrated. It could be the friend who is always the center of everyone's attention.

Jealousy keeps us on a perpetual quest for the attention, affection, and affirmation of others.

Jealousy once again pricks the "I am not enough" fear. Comparison leads us to realize we might not measure up, and jealousy affirms our fear by identifying the person who might become the honored one. Jealousy leads us to believe that someone else will be better and therefore steal the attention and interest of those we revere.

Jealousy keeps us on a perpetual quest for the attention, affection, and affirmation of others. We're constantly comparing ourselves to others, and if someone has something we lack, jealousy starts strategizing about how to get it back.

In Proverbs 27:4 we read, "Anger is cruel and fury overwhelming, / but who can stand before jealousy?" Jealousy is like a cancer that eats away at everything that is good in our relationships. Influence is earned through relationships. Position can give us power for a time, but only relationships can give us lasting influence. When jealousy drives us, our ability to develop strong relationships is hindered. In our protective, defensive stance our influence decreases rather than increases.

Cain killed his brother, Abel. Jacob robbed Esau of his birthright. Rachel and Leah lived at odds with each other. Saul put out a death warrant on David's life. In each of these stories jealousy took root and ruined their relationships.

Jealousy becomes more sophisticated as we mature, and its root system is strengthened with every episode in which we allow it to flourish. It begins with our natural competition and comparison as siblings, and it grows rather aggressively as we jockey for position on our school sports team or in the drama club. But perhaps it's the most devious when it sneaks into our professional relationships.

I have always prided myself on being the teacher's pet. All my insecurities and fears are assuaged for a moment when I have the favor of someone I esteem with power. I also have an unhealthy affection for hierarchy. Perhaps it's because I prefer order and structure, but I fear it's more likely because it helps me find a way to measure my worth. The farther up the ladder I go, the more confident I feel. This unhealthy affection tempts me to idolize those in the highest levels of leadership while disregarding those whom I've surpassed. As long as I'm in the good graces and favor of those I revere, things are pleasant. As soon as someone threatens my position, jealousy runs fierce.

JEALOUSY IMPACTS OUR INFLUENCE

Jealousy is an attribute that we as leaders are not quick to acknowledge in our lives. It feels petty and juvenile. We hope that we've outgrown jealousy along with acne and all-nighters. But we don't grow out of jealousy naturally; it's an element of emotional and spiritual health that needs deliberate attention. Left unrecognized it might be silently undermining your influence, as it was for me.

Jealousy might show up when

- someone else is recognized for a job well done.
- a friend chooses to confide in someone else rather than in you.
- your child prefers to spend more time with your ex.
- an employee seeks counsel from another leader.
- your spouse enjoys a rare night out with friends rather than a night at home with you.

Jealousy makes other people—even people we like and respect—our enemies. The "I am not enough" fear launches us into a battle for position and affirmation of our worth. A *Harvard Business Review* article cited the story of two colleagues, Scott and Marty, who were initially good friends and strong teammates. Then jealousy started to affect their working relationship: "Although Marty was objectively the stronger performer, Scott's personality and social network earned him more attention, opportunities, and recognition both inside and outside the firm. At first, Marty brushed aside his resentment, telling himself that people would inevitably recognize his superiority. However, as Scott's charm catapulted him higher, Marty's envy won out."[2] Marty began undermining Scott, distancing himself and disengaging from the organization. His passion for work deteriorated, and his performance suffered. Ultimately he left the organization.

Jealousy is an uncomfortable clout killer to admit because it feeds on our emotional vulnerabilities. The *Harvard Business Review* article helped explain our resistance to acknowledging how jealousy or envy is impacting us by saying it "is difficult to manage, in part because it's hard to admit that we harbor such a socially unacceptable emotion. Our discomfort causes us to conceal and deny our feelings, and that makes things worse."[3] Sometimes simple comparison leads us to the trail of jealousy, but we can be the most vulnerable to becoming jealous when other issues are hidden under the surface. Two underlying issues often trigger jealousy:

1. LACK OF SECURITY

When you don't feel secure, you will be defensive and territorial. Your chief focus becomes protecting yourself. In an effort to protect yourself you may subconsciously assume that everyone is out to get you. This lack of security could be triggered by a previous job loss, childhood circumstances, or unhealthy relationships. Whatever the reason for your feeling unsafe and insecure, you allow room for jealousy to impact your relationships if you don't acknowledge this underlying trigger.

2. Lack of Trust

Lack of trust in another person can also be a trigger for jealousy. If you don't trust the intentions of the other person, you will always question his actions. You will be suspicious of his motives and find it impossible to believe the best about him.

I learned that the words *envy* and *jealousy* aren't necessarily interchangeable. A *New York Times* article reported, "Envy involves a longing for what you don't have, while jealousy is provoked by losing something to someone else."[4] Pastor Robert Morris clarified it this way: "We're jealous of people. We're envious of things."[5] The distinction is in losing versus longing. Jealousy at its core is the fear of losing something or someone, while envy is the aching longing for what we don't have.

Jealousy and envy feed the "I am not enough" fear. Jealousy says, "I'm not enough, but I need to make sure that no one else is better." Envy says, "I'm not enough because I don't have the things that would make me enough."

Envy is an endless longing with no possibility of satisfaction. Just think about a typical day for a minute. You pry yourself out of bed, wishing you had a job that allowed you to control your schedule. Your plans to go to the gym are thwarted because of the extra thirty minutes you slept in because you were up in the middle of the night calming your youngest child after a bad dream. You envy those who have time for regular exercise and the fit physique that accompanies their routine. As you, your spouse, the kids, and the dog jockey for territory while you make breakfast and scramble out the door, you grumble about needing a bigger home. As you are pulling out of the driveway, you notice the check engine light that has been on for a week reminding you of that new car you've been hoping to get, but you haven't been able to swing the payment. As you pull into the office a few minutes late, you envy the idea of a life that isn't so exhausting.

Proverbs 14:30 sums it up: "A heart at peace gives life to the body, / but envy rots the bones." Death, decay, despair—envy eat away at us. Envy quickly becomes a runaway train in our lives; it's tied to comparison and our American cultural norm to keep up with the Joneses and live above our means in an attempt to look good. It was our circle of friends in middle school, our accomplishments in high school, the college where we got accepted, the fiancé we lassoed, the job we landed, the family we built, the monster house, the luxury car, on and on it goes. We always long for something that someone else has. And it's not just stuff. It's looks, personality, lifestyle, choices, and attitudes. We constantly wish to be someone other than who we are.

Our constant longing robs us of finding peace with who we are and being content with the work we've been given.

No wonder the Bible says that it rots our bones. It eats us to the core of who we are. It kills our clout. Our constant longing robs us of finding peace with who we are and being content with the work *we've* been given. Envy is one of the greatest distractions to our influence. It takes our focus off our opportunities for influence and tempts us to fixate on everyone else's.

CONFRONTING JEALOUSY AND ENVY

I'm generally a fan of social media. I actively use Facebook, Twitter, Instagram, and Pinterest. I enjoy meeting new people, sharing thoughts and ideas, and having a forum to chatter about the simple things. However, the dark side of social media may be the format to perpetuate the sins of envy and comparison. Social media by nature only give space for us to put our best foot forward. Our most aspirational self is portrayed, while our fears, challenges, and unmet desires remain hidden. After all, who wants to willingly follow a constant critic or an endless stream of depressing thoughts?

Envy becomes social competition. We envy and compare what is good about others' lives while they envy what is good about ours. We share only what is great in our lives for fear of being less than someone else.

One way that we begin to combat envy is to realize that the grass is never greener. We have to accept that we see only a portion of someone else's world. The person whom you think has it all really doesn't. Perfection is an illusion; there is more to every story. Envying only the best moments is an insult to your process of discovering your clout as well as others'. When you fixate on the influence of others, you neglect discovering and unleashing your own. You neglect the sphere of influence in front of you as you idolize another's.

Our obsession with loss and our longings for more do significant damage to our influence. Jealousy and envy wreak havoc on us in three key ways.

1. Splintered Relationships

Jealousy and envy drive an enormous wedge between people in relationships. How could they not? Both are birthed out of comparison of yourself to others. They form a divide between who gained and who lost, between who has and who has not. They horribly distort and twist our relationships into endless competition and comparison rather than life-giving community. Leader and author Nancy Beach commented on this issue:

> What most concerns me about envy in the hearts of . . . leaders is that it wastes so much of our time, robs us of deep joy in our own uniqueness, and destroys the possibility for authentic and life-giving community. Our coveting creates distance between us and God and between us and others. When I am envious, I can't be truly grateful or productive because I am too busy feeling deprived.[6]

Envy and jealousy splinter trust and cause us to live guarded lives. As leaders, we invite distrust and guardedness to be a part of the culture when we allow envy or jealousy into our relationships with those we influence. We believe that we're good at hiding these clout killers, but we're not. We're only fooling ourselves. We have to understand the impact of these unresolved issues on those we lead.

Our leadership and influence are all about relationships. If we as leaders struggle with the sins of jealousy and envy, they will impact those we

Envy and jealousy splinter trust and cause us to live guarded lives.

lead. Jealousy and envy cause us to covet the clout of someone else and miss the significance of our contribution. When that happens, we all lose. We fixate on what we don't have and harbor resentment toward others who have the influence we desire. In doing this we neglect to develop the clout for which we've been created. We do not develop our opportunities for influence, and we create distance between us and those we envy.

2. NEGATIVE MULTIPLICATION

The apostle James made strong statements about the dangers of envy: "If you harbor bitter envy and selfish ambition in your hearts, do not boast about it or deny the truth. . . . For where you have envy and selfish ambition, there you find disorder and every evil practice" (James 3:14, 16).

Envy and jealousy are destructive to our souls. They are like poison that permeates our thought processes and inhibits healthy things from growing and maturing. When we allow them to take root, we make way for evil to impact our influence. The word *evil* makes me uncomfortable. I understand that jealousy and envy are not good. I recognize the places where they run rampant in my life, but *evil*?

Perhaps an example of how evil shows up is our secret celebration when someone we envy fails. When a rival botches a project, loses a job, or encounters a setback, we silently cheer because we've just gained ground on her. I know that feels uncomfortable to admit, but the only way we begin to step into all that God has desired for us is to identify the enemies that are holding us back.

I think James said it so strongly because he was trying to get our attention. Jealousy and envy are dangerous to our souls. They are dangerous to the clout that God is calling us to develop. When we allow envy and jealousy to impact our influence, they in turn impact those we lead. Just as jealous sibling rivalry passed from Jacob and Esau to Rachel and Leah and in turn to Joseph and his brothers, jealousy and envy are sins that multiply and carry forward. The longer these patterns continue, the more limited our influence will become.

3. UNGRATEFUL ATTITUDES

Never enough. Ultimately jealousy and envy cause us to live in perpetual discontentment. Nothing is ever enough.

I lead a very blessed life. Of course I've had my share of ups and downs, but overall I'm extraordinarily blessed. All it takes is a trip to the slums of Kolkata, India, on one of our Cross Point mission trips, and I am reminded of my extravagant blessings.

But there have been seasons when I have been gripped by embarrassing discontentment. Discontentment so fierce that I've been tempted to walk away from all of it because none of it was good enough anyway. As much as I try to be attractive, intelligent, kind, generous, purposeful, and significant, I never measure up to whomever I have idealized for that specific affirmation. I'll never be the leader that John Maxwell is. I'll never be the beauty that Duchess Kate is. I'll never be the speaker that Andy Stanley is. I'll never be as outgoing as my friend Eve. I'll never be . . .

"I'll never be" thoughts do not allow me to realize what I am. "I'll never be" thoughts lead to a place of deep ungratefulness and discontentment. Ungratefulness and discontentment are dangerous to my clout and gravely insult my God who has provided all my needs (Phil. 4:19) and "knit me together in my mother's womb" (Ps. 139:13), my God who has a specific plan and purpose for my life (Jer. 29:11) that he is longing for me to discover!

The enemy of our souls is always looking for a distraction. When he can keep us focused on what we don't have rather than on what we do have, he knows that our ability to live out God's purpose and plan is severely diminished. Envy and jealousy are two extraordinary tools that he uses to keep us off a proper focus. The damage that can be done to our relationships, the patterns that are developed, and the festering ungratefulness distract us from confidently stepping into our place of leadership and influence.

Exchanging Jealousy and Envy for Affirmation and Celebration

The antidote to jealousy and envy is to replace them with affirmation and celebration of the influence of others. Jealousy and envy tempt us to diminish the worth of others. The best way to combat the negative progression of these clout killers is to go the opposite direction by affirming and celebrating the influence of others.

Celebrating others involves pointing out their strengths and telling them what they mean to you and the organization. It means seeking their input on issues, especially when they have an area of expertise that you lack. Celebrating others is publicly acknowledging people for jobs well done. It means speaking into people's strengths and gifts and encouraging them to keep developing them.

With an attitude of celebration, we take the focus off ourselves and begin to find value in what others bring. The irony of celebrating others' gifts is that we actually begin to find more value in our own.

My assistant, Ashley, has worked with me more than seven

years in various capacities. She is gifted in numerous ways, but what I value most about her is her gift of harmony. Ashley is a peacekeeper. She is very sensitive to how the team is getting along. She knows instinctively who is happy, who is discouraged, who is stressed, and who is thriving. In my drivenness I have a tendency to miss many cues that she picks up on. I used to beat myself up over my insensitivity and felt defeated because I didn't have the same awareness that she did. Over time, however, I have learned that her strengths in this area are a perfect complement to mine and a valuable gift that allows us to work well together. Apart, neither one of us would serve the rest of the team as effectively as we do together.

Once I learned the value of celebrating Ashley's gift rather than envying it, I became even more effective in my leadership. Although I'll never be as sensitive to others' needs as she is, I can improve my influence with the rest of the team by asking for her insight and opinion. Whenever I'm about to make a big decision or lead through a season of change, I invite Ashley into the conversation and hear her perspective on how it will impact the team.

Note that the absence of a gift is not permission to dismiss its importance. My lack of sensitivity is not permission to be insensitive. Awareness of a gap in my gifts is an opportunity for me to seek out someone who is strong in that area to complement my weakness.

Celebrating others' gifts is a distinct choice that you must make. It chips away at your temptation to constantly envy them. You'll find joy and freedom in celebrating rather than comparing. By choosing to celebrate and affirm others, you stop the sins of envy and jealousy from creeping in.

Another important point about celebrating others is that it's contagious. When you start celebrating others, they will in turn begin celebrating others too. You will start to experience a positive shift in the culture, and unity will permeate the team.

When we become confident and comfortable in our God-given influence, we can begin to put an end to jealousy and envy and focus on further development of ourselves and others. That's clout.

DISCOVERY STEPS

- Do you wrestle more with jealousy or envy?
- Is there someone in your life of whom you are regularly jealous? What could you do to begin championing that person?
- What are you most tempted to envy? How could you take your focus off what you lack and find gratefulness in what you have?

CHAPTER 4

YOU HAVE ENOUGH

Squeezing Out Scarcity

People with a scarcity mentality tend to see everything in terms of "win-lose." They believe "There is only so much; and if someone else has it, that means there will be less for me."

—STEPHEN R. COVEY[1]

WILL THERE BE ENOUGH? IT WAS AN HONEST AND sincere question that was asked almost daily at my home when I was growing up. I was born in a blue-collar small town in northern Wisconsin where living was rather lean. Factory layoffs were common occurrences, and minimum wage was the best you could expect when you were working. Making ends meet was challenging, and my parents found it impossible to shelter me from that reality.

My early life experience with scarcity taught me valuable

lessons. It taught me to take care of what I had and to maximize everything. I took very little for granted because I knew what it meant not to have it. I learned the value of hard work, and I experienced the payoff of reaping the rewards of a little sweat equity. Nothing was more fulfilling than toiling with my grandmother throughout the summer to plant, water, weed, and harvest our garden, which provided hundreds of jars of vegetables to last us through the winter.

Scarcity also taught me to treasure new things. My family was wonderful at celebrating birthdays and Christmases. Somehow my parents always managed to make those days special. While the in-between times were marked by memories of scarcity, birthdays and Christmases carry precious memories of thoughtful gifts and special treasures.

But scarcity also taught me darker things. It taught me to hoard, protect, and defend. It taught me to be skeptical. It taught me to play it safe and minimize risk. At times it has robbed me of having a generous heart, and it has often convinced me that I'm all on my own. It has even led me to believe that no one else cares and to question whether God is really there.

Those things are dangerous enough when they impact only me, but that's the problem with life as a leader—none of my issues impact just me. Every issue that we wrestle with as leaders impacts those we influence. A mindset of scarcity impacts how I react to, serve, and lead others. This thought pattern affects every action I take. If I'm not purposeful to sort out the good and the bad, I will pass on the good *and the bad* to those I lead.

> *Every issue that we wrestle with as leaders impacts those we influence.*

In her book *Daring Greatly,* author and social researcher Brené Brown lists a series of questions that will help you discern whether scarcity impacts your influence:

Is self-worth tied to achievement, productivity, or compliance?

Is perfectionism an issue?

[Is] there constant overt or covert comparing and ranking?

Are people held to one narrow standard rather than acknowledged for their unique gifts and contributions?

Is there an ideal way of being or one form of talent that is used as measurement of everyone else's worth?

Are people afraid to take risks or try new things?[2]

If any of those questions indicate how you feel or how the culture of your team feels, it's possible that scarcity is impacting your influence.

SCARCITY IMPACTS OUR INFLUENCE

Scarcity begins to grip us when we're confronted with the fear that there may not be enough. When we fear not having enough, we begin to fiercely hoard and protect what we can control. Scarcity turns our focus inward, and we become fixated on survival.

If you've ever been in a situation where you desperately needed something for survival that wasn't available, you may have a true understanding of scarcity. Perhaps it was food or water, medical attention or lifesaving medication. Absence of these items can be terrifying when they mean life or death.

The response to scarcity may very well be a God-given instinct in our literal survival. If that has been your experience, I don't intend to diminish the true fear of need that you've experienced. That's not the type of scarcity we're talking about here.

Sometimes an honest experience of scarcity can impact how you perceive everything. I first realized scarcity was a mind-set that was driving my actions when I was promoted to a role that included directly managing other staff members. After a few short weeks of managing a new employee, I was extraordinarily frustrated and feeling defeated. My employee was a bright, competent individual, but her efforts were never enough for me. There was always a bit more that she could have done. There was always room for improvement or a way to accomplish a task more efficiently. My self-worth became tied not only to my accomplishments but also to hers. I subconsciously believed that her performance was a direct reflection on me. I felt pressure for my performance and hers to be perfect.

Scarcity was an honest experience for me in my early years, yet I had unknowingly allowed it to become a mind-set that developed into a type of paranoia. I was terrified of never having enough. Scarcity becomes a clout killer when we carry it into everyday life. Susan Jeffers describes people with scarcity fears this way:

> They are imbued with a deep-seated sense of scarcity in the world, as if there wasn't enough to go around. Not enough love, not enough money, not enough praise, not enough attention—simply not enough. Usually fear in one area of our lives generalizes, and we become closed down and protective in many areas of our lives.[3]

Scarcity in this context is birthed from an unnecessary fear that causes us to live and lead with the fear that if we give more, we won't have enough.

Scarcity subconsciously causes us to lead from two dangerous perspectives:

1. It's all about me.
2. I need more.

It's All About Me

When we believe that there is not enough to go around, we live guarded, territorial, and self-focused lives. We view the world from a protective posture, often assuming that others are out to get us.

One of the most important lessons we have to learn about unleashing our God-given influence is that it is not simply for our benefit. It is for God's plan and purpose to be accomplished through us for the blessing of others. A mind-set of scarcity gets in the way of that influence because it keeps us focused on ourselves and what we lack. In our hoarding and protecting we take our focus off using our influence for others.

I've seen this dynamic play out numerous times in the workplace. A manager who is fearful of losing his position of influence limits the opportunities he creates for his staff. He sparingly invites employees to meetings and maintains tight control on how information is dispersed. Fearful that his peers or employees could take his place, he is slow to acknowledge their efforts or to offer feedback or praise. His greatest concern is protecting himself.

A survey by the American Psychological Association reported, "Just 52 percent of employees said they feel valued on the job,

[and] only two-thirds reported being motivated to do their best at work."[4] Additional discussion and research on these findings suggest that unhealthy managers are a primary reason for employees feeling undervalued and unfulfilled.[5]

> *When leaders manage from a position of scarcity, they create unhealthy environments for those they influence.*

When leaders manage from a position of scarcity, they create unhealthy environments for those they influence. Rather than focus on developing and investing in others, we focus on protecting and defending ourselves. Stewarding our influence is impossible from a position of scarcity because our actions are motivated by self-preservation.

I Need More

Because scarcity taps your fear of not having enough, nothing is ever enough. You always see the potential for something to be better. Scarcity creates an insatiable quest for more.

Let me tell you how this has played out in my life. I am generally a good person. I always have been. Sure I've had a mischievous moment or two and I've certainly logged my list of sins, but as human measurement goes, I'm a good person. I try to do the right things and please the ones who matter. My desire to be good takes me down a trail toward perfection that I have never quite attained. Although I have accomplished good things, I am never, ever satisfied. I set goals, achieve them, receive praise, and still brush it off as not quite enough. Even in accomplishing some of my greatest dreams, I have walked away feeling unfulfilled. It's scarcity at work in my heart. In spite of doing things that I've always dreamed, every day I fear that it will all disappear.

My spouse will leave me. My boss will fire me. My family will disown me. My employees will revolt against me. My safety will be threatened by a crisis. My friends will walk away. My health will be compromised.

My scarcity mind-set has caused me to live most of my life with a gnawing fear that it will all disappear if I don't do everything I can to keep gathering it. Gather more praise and affirmation. Gather more love. Gather more accolades. Gather more awards. Gather more friends. Gather more and more and more.

But the more I gather, the less I give. How could I give more when it's taking all my energy to gather? When we gather rather than give, we erode our influence with others. We impair clout rather than earn it.

Consider how this plays out with my expectations of others. My insatiable quest for more becomes an overwhelming burden to those in my sphere of influence. I become impossible to please. My spouse never does quite enough, whether it's completing projects around the house or spending time with me. Those I lead feel that they can never meet my impossible expectations. No matter how well they finish a project or how successfully they manage an event, I always have feedback for improvement. Nothing is ever enough.

In my constant push for more, I actually push everyone away. Once again my influence is impacted but not for the positive.

Can you see tendencies of this in your life? Do your children feel that they can never measure up? Does your spouse feel like a servant at times? Do the volunteers or staff you lead feel defeated when you give feedback?

Scarcity is another clout killer that may be impacting your influence whether you fully realize it or not. Now that we understand a bit more of what it looks like and where it could be coming from, let's look at how we can allow scarcity to impact our influence through our words, our time, and our opportunities.

OUR WORDS

A couple of years ago, my sister and I were spending a pleasant Friday afternoon together when she received a terrifying call from a friend. Trying to decipher her frantic words as she raced to her car, I interpreted that her apartment was on fire. We arrived in time to see flames shooting out of her apartment, and we watched in horror as all her possessions and her precious dog were lost that day. The loss and destruction still haunt us.

A small spark in the form of a frustrated reaction or an insensitive comment can create a blaze of destruction in the hearts of those we lead.

The apostle James cautioned that our words can carry the same intensity and destruction of a raging fire: "The tongue is a small part of the body, but it makes great boasts. Consider what a great forest can be set on fire by a small spark. The tongue also is a fire, a world of evil among the parts of the body. It corrupts the whole body, sets the whole course of one's life on fire, and is itself set on fire by hell" (James 3:5–6).

Every time I read that passage, I shudder. How many times have my words caused harm? When we believe that nothing is ever enough, our mouths can't help saying so. Scarcity overrides our sensitivity and causes us to spew sparks. When nothing is ever enough, we are quick to complain about it. Our frantic fears cause us to say things that we later wish we could retract. A small spark in the form of a frustrated reaction or an insensitive comment can create a blaze of destruction in the hearts of those we lead.

I'm ashamed of the number of times I have discouraged a friend, a family member, a coworker, or an employee with an insensitive comment. When I am focused more on my fears born of scarcity than on the importance of the people around me, I am managing my influence poorly and making self-serving choices.

Scarcity also shows up in the words we don't say. I've discovered my tendency to withhold good words. Although I'm quick to speak frustration or discouragement, I'm not always as quick to speak words of encouragement and praise. Words of support and affirmation don't flow as freely. Scarcity causes us to withhold good words because we're afraid that whatever we praise won't continue for long. Because our fear is that there's not enough, we are tempted to believe that if we praise someone else, the praise somehow takes away from who we are. This clout killer has convinced me that if I encourage you, I become less valuable.

OUR TIME

When we live with the fear that there is not enough, time is an extra-scarce commodity. There are never enough hours in a day. Our to-do list always exceeds the hours that we allocate to it. We live in a perpetual state of feeling behind.

And leaders with a scarce perspective of time can wear down the people around us. In our attempts to manipulate and control time so as to work most effectively for ourselves, we place additional stress on others who need to meet our time expectations.

In his best-selling book *Getting Things Done*, David Allen describes the challenge in having enough time: "Almost everyone I encounter these days feels he or she has too much to handle and not enough time to get it done." He adds, "A paradox has emerged in this new millennium: people have enhanced quality of life, but at the same time they are adding to their stress levels by taking on more than they have resources to handle. It's as though their eyes were bigger than their stomachs. And most people are to some degree frustrated and perplexed about how to improve the situation."[6]

Leaders who fear that there will not be enough lead with a sense of urgency. Every project time line is a little more aggressive than the last one. Every deadline is created with the slimmest margins. If we completed the annual report in four weeks last year, surely we can do it in three weeks this year. If we launched the last project in six months, five should be fine this time.

Leaders who lead this way leave no time for people to catch their breath. While you may believe that you can maintain such an aggressive pace, it's insensitive to assume that others can handle that and not burn out.

The other challenge of time scarcity is that we minimize our time and attention devoted to others. Time scarcity can lead to being task focused instead of people focused. Driven by the clock, we value performance over time spent with those we lead and influence. I quickly see this happen in my leadership. When a large project is on my plate, I squeeze out any available margin. Rather than leave thirty-minute breaks between meetings, I cram them back-to-back, abruptly stopping and starting to keep up with the pace of my agenda. In doing so I eliminate the margin for conversations to go longer if necessary or for me to take a stroll through the office to say hello and encourage the team.

When the constraint of time directs my behavior, I begin sacrificing the value of the relationships. Everyone in my life becomes bound by my calendar, and rather than be a life-giving leader, I become a stressed-out taskmaster.

OUR OPPORTUNITIES

The real task of leadership is giving it away. As your clout increases, so do your opportunities to be the one up front. As you discover and unleash your God-given influence, you will be given more and more opportunities to lead others. Scarcity tells you that you need to save the best opportunities for yourself. *You* must be in the spotlight. *You* must give the presentation. *You* must lead the meeting. *You* must give the instructions. *You* must share the good news.

Because we're afraid of missing opportunities for ourselves, scarcity challenges us to perceive others as a threat. Scarcity withholds opportunities from others because we don't want to give up the opportunity for ourselves. We limit others' potential to grow because we're afraid of being overlooked.

> *The real test of leadership and influence is when we're willing to stand behind others and let them shine.*

The real test of leadership and influence is when we're willing to stand behind others and let them shine. It's not that there aren't strategic moments when your specific gifts will require you to be the person up front, but the test is whether you can give up the limelight. John Maxwell defends his leadership Law of Reproduction with the argument that "more than four out of five of all the leaders that you ever meet will have emerged as leaders because of the impact made on them by established leaders who mentored them."[7]

Remember, scarcity causes us to hoard and protect. That includes our opportunities. If as leaders, we're unwilling to give opportunities to others, we may be allowing scarcity to inhibit our influence. What staff member could you ask to lead a meeting to help her develop her leadership gifts? What friend could you invite to teach the small-group lesson? What coworker could you partner with on a new project?

CONFRONTING SCARCITY

Do you see times in your life when you've been scarce with your words, your time, or your opportunities? Perhaps this discussion has triggered other areas where you have a tendency to hoard and protect.

The underlying danger with scarcity is that it maintains distance between you and others. By withholding words of encouragement, you will miss out on the opportunities to build relationships with the people you influence. By allowing your schedule to be so demanding, you will shortchange your team of time for development. And by refusing to give others the opportunity to lead a meeting or chair a project, you will limit their growth potential. Scarcity holds you back and hinders you from leading sincerely and authentically. It will keep you from doing the creative best with the work that God has given you to do.

For me, scarcity boils down to the fear that there will never be enough. Although my scarcity roots were planted in my youth when resources were limited, those experiences were not the full picture. In Philippians 4:19 Paul reminded us of this promise: "My God will meet all your needs according to the riches of his glory in Christ Jesus."

God will provide all our needs. What if we really believed that? Scarcity teaches us to fend for ourselves. The idea that God will provide contradicts our scarcity instincts. This is where we must confront scarcity with truth. If God's Word is true, our scarcity fears are not. If God will provide all our needs, there *is* enough. God is enough, and God will provide enough. When we recognize that who God has created us to be and the work he has given us to do are enough, we can lay aside our attempts at hoarding and protecting and trust everything to his care.

And let's be honest, scarcity doesn't impact our influence in the things that are necessary for survival. Our words, our time, and our opportunities are rarely in limited supply, especially if we choose to be generous with them.

Faith comes in here. We have to choose to believe what God says and alter our perspective accordingly. If we believe that everything is limited and there will never be enough, we will always lead from that state of mind. It is a belief that we have the ability to choose. We can choose scarcity or we can choose faith. If we believe that God does supply all our needs and he will provide, we must replace our fear with faith and open up and start giving generously.

EXCHANGING SCARCITY FOR GENEROSITY

To overcome our fear of scarcity, we have to replace it with a spirit of generosity. We must respond with the exact opposite of our natural tendency. Rather than hoard, we must give. In an article for *Forbes*, author Erika Andersen described the significance of generosity:

> Generosity evokes generosity: when someone supports you, acknowledges you, offers you their belief and faith—it makes you want to reciprocate in kind. I've noticed that leaders who practice generosity create teams where information flows more freely; people reach beyond their job descriptions to support each other; team members celebrate each others' successes.[8]

Generous leaders are contagious. Generosity multiplies our clout. Our God-given influence thrives and blesses others.

Our generosity shows up in the same ways that scarcity did—through our words, our time, and our opportunities.

GENEROUS WITH WORDS

Remember James's strong words about our words? That our words can be a spark for evil? Although there is no doubt that our words can be evil sparks, our words can also spark a number of good things. Consider these reminders in Scripture:

> *The words of the reckless pierce like swords,*
> *but the tongue of the wise brings healing.*
> (PROV. 12:18)

> *Gracious words are a honeycomb,*
> *sweet to the soul and healing to the bones.*
> (PROV. 16:24)

The soothing tongue is a tree of life,
but a perverse tongue crushes the spirit.
(PROV. 15:4)

Encourage one another and build each other up.
(1THESS. 5:11)

The mouths of the righteous utter wisdom,
and their tongues speak what is just.
(PS. 37:30)

Do not let any unwholesome talk come out of your mouths, but
only what is helpful for building others up according to their
needs, that it may benefit those who listen.
(EPH. 4:29)

There is power in our words—both in words spoken and in words withheld. Perhaps you are not destructive with your words and you're not lighting blazing fires with your insensitivity, but what might you be holding back? Where could a word fitly spoken create a spark of comfort and encouragement? Where could you ignite a blaze of hope and potential in those you influence? Who needs to hear that you're proud of him or her? Who needs to know that you're grateful for what they do? Who needs to hear that you understand and that you are praying for them? Who needs to know what you specifically value about their gifts and contribution? Where could your words change a life because you choose to exchange scarcity for generosity?

> *There is power in our words—both in words spoken and in words withheld.*

GENEROUS WITH TIME

What about your time? How can you be more generous with the time and attention you invest in others? I know it might seem disingenuous, but if you struggle with being task focused and starve others of your time, you may need to purposefully schedule it into your week.

One of my bosses in the early days of my career walked the halls and visited all our cubicles every morning. I was really intrigued (and honestly sometimes annoyed) by this habit. I figured he had plenty to do. It seemed a very casual way to approach his day. When I asked him about it, he explained that he made himself do it as a way to be available to the staff before he got too tied up in projects. He made it a very deliberate part of his schedule because he knew his task-oriented nature would keep him from engaging with the team otherwise.

I've never forgotten that lesson. While I might have been mildly annoyed because I thought he was checking on us first thing every morning, he was actually being purposeful about making time for his staff.

If you have a tendency to be scarce with your time, how can you make more time for the people in your sphere of influence? Do you need to carve out time in your weekly schedule for a stroll through the office? Perhaps you can keep one day a week open for a spontaneous lunch meeting with someone who needs a bit of extra time with you. How can you be more purposeful to tidy up your work before you leave the office so that you're not sending one more e-mail or making one more call when you get home? Can you reserve an hour every Friday morning for a phone call to a friend or a family member?

We're all bound by the constraints of time. If you have a

tendency to view time through a scarcity lens, you will need to reshape your priorities and allow scheduled time and attention for those you feel most called to serve with your God-given influence. We build into our lives what is important to our hearts, so here's a hint: schedule time with God first, your family second, and then your job, your friends, and your other activities in the priority order that makes best sense for you.

GENEROUS WITH OPPORTUNITIES

This might be the most difficult one: being generous with opportunities. In other words giving power away. It's the old leadership cliché "Give up to go up." As you grow in leadership, you must give up some opportunities to emerging leaders. If you hoard all the opportunities, you're not a leader. You're a dictator. If keeping the power to yourself is your preference, your influence will forever be limited.

I'll be honest. This is difficult to get right. There are certain opportunities and experiences that you need to have, but there are others that you need to give away. A great way to start is by bringing others with you. Who in your sphere of influence has potential that you would like to develop? Where can they come along to watch and learn from you? Who can you invite to colead the next committee meeting or special event?

> *If keeping the power to yourself is your preference, your influence will forever be limited.*

Another way to be generous with opportunities is to look for ways to make connections. Does someone in your circle of influence have great respect for another leader you know? Make the introduction. Would one of your staff members be an asset to a company-wide project? Instead of being fearful of the project taking time away from the work she does for you, generously offer for her to be involved.

Whenever you feel a tinge of scarcity impacting your decisions, you have to stop and think of a way to flip that perception on its head and do something generous. Scarcity may have a limited place when it teaches the value of stewardship, much like my early years did. I would never trade my season of lack because it taught me to be grateful for blessings. Scarcity never has a place, however, when it means hoarding and protecting our words, our time, and our opportunities from blessing and benefiting others. When we choose generosity over scarcity, we're free to love, support, and champion others. We begin to realize that God's provision is enough, and out of that overflow our clout begins to thrive!

DISCOVERY STEPS

- Do you struggle with scarcity? If you do, where do you think your mind-set of scarcity originated?
- Are you more tempted to hoard your words, your time, or your opportunities?
- What are two things you could do to be more generous in this area?

CHAPTER 5

YOU ARE GOOD ENOUGH

Identifying Insecurity

It's insecurity that is always chasing you and standing in the way of your dreams.

—Vin Diesel[1]

TIM WAS ONE OF THE MOST BRILLIANT PEOPLE I've ever worked with. He had amazing ideas, a great work ethic, passion, and conviction, but insecurity got the best of him. Constant growth and change repeatedly provided challenges for all of us, but Tim just couldn't get comfortable with them. The success of the company required quick response. Deadlines were tight and the workload had to be outsourced to keep up with the demands. Several times our boss took a project that would ordinarily be assigned to Tim and me and gave it to another team in order to spread out the workload.

This often pricked my insecurities, too, but Tim came unglued. Whenever a project was taken away from him, he regarded it as a personal attack. No matter how well our boss explained the situation and reinforced his belief in him, Tim reacted defensively. New staff members were added, and our team was expanded. That meant that every one of us had to divide our workloads and give up a part of our jobs. But Tim couldn't shake the fear that somehow he was not doing enough and all these changes and additions were an indictment of his performance rather than an outcome of our success.

Instead of being the thriving, contributing team member that he had always been, Tim turned into a defensive, territorial, and reclusive team member. Despite numerous conversations, pep talks, and encouragement from our boss, Tim couldn't shake his insecurities about the changes; he eventually resigned.

In contrast, Rebecca, who was another team member, saw the changes as an opportunity to grow. Rather than perceive the new members as threats, she embraced them as people to invest in. Confident in her knowledge and abilities, she contributed her best to the team while strategically helping bring out the best in everyone else. She was helpful. She was engaged. She was committed. It's no surprise that Rebecca continued to be promoted and given even greater opportunities to lead.

If you are like me and don't like the word *insecurity*, you might prefer to think of it as the state of not being confident. Insecurity can strike even the most confident leader. I suspect most of us can relate to not feeling confident from time to time. Not confident in our ideas, our abilities, our gifts, our talents, our dreams, our relationships, our purpose, our significance.

Momentary lack of confidence is rather normal. Whenever we're confronted with something that will stretch us, change us, or grow us, we're likely to feel a level of insecurity.

Your clout becomes compromised when you experience a perpetual lack of confidence. Insecurity is sparked by fear and antagonized by doubt. Insecurity causes us once again to wrestle with the "I am not enough" fear.

Not good enough, strong enough, smart enough, kind enough, beautiful enough, witty enough, creative enough, "you fill in the blank" enough. Fear raises the question,

> *Your clout becomes compromised when you experience a perpetual lack of confidence.*

comparison measures how we stack up to others, jealousy counts what we stand to lose, scarcity makes us defensive, and insecurity begins to unravel any ounce of confidence we have left. One psychologist defined *insecurity* in these terms:

> Insecurity refers to a profound sense of self-doubt—a deep feeling of uncertainty about our basic worth and our place in the world. Insecurity is associated with chronic self-consciousness, along with a chronic lack of confidence in ourselves and anxiety about our relationships. The insecure man or woman lives in constant fear of rejection and a deep uncertainty about whether his or her own feelings and desires are legitimate.[2]

The phrases that make up this definition are significant. Each one on its own could send you into hours of counseling! These descriptors of insecurity give structure to a clout killer that is sometimes difficult to identify in our lives:

- profound sense of self-doubt
- uncertainty about our basic worth and place in the world
- chronic self-consciousness
- chronic lack of confidence
- anxiety about our relationships
- fear of rejection
- uncertainty about whether our feelings and desires are legitimate

Do they hit a nerve? Can you see moments in your life and leadership where you have been burdened by one, two, or all of these feelings? Insecurity doesn't feel so petty by this definition. These are sensitive questions that sting in the deepest places of the soul.

This list makes me feel as if someone is reading my journals. These are the things I rarely feel comfortable sharing with another person. I feel as if I'm somehow giving power to them if I speak them. If it's true when they say, "Ignorance is bliss," maybe it's better to ignore them and pretend they're not there.

Most of us don't begin recognizing the impact of our insecurities on our influence until we have influence for them to impact.

And how would my influence as a leader be compromised if I gave voice to these issues? This list of insecurities doesn't seem to describe the character of a leader. Before long I've become insecure about my insecurities.

In my experience, most of us don't begin recognizing the impact of our insecurities on our influence until we have influence for them to impact. In other words, we recognize the danger of our insecurities when something is at risk.

Warren G. Harding has the notorious reputation of being one of the worst presidents of the United States. His legacy of scandal and corruption is commonly attributed to the intense insecurity that drove him to show favoritism and avoid responsibility. He is said to have privately shared, "I am not fit for this office [of president] and should never have been here."[3]

How does someone with an enormous position of influence such as Harding's succumb to the clout killer of insecurity? I suspect that rather than deal with insecurity, Harding attempted to keep covering it up until his influence had grown to a level where he could no longer mask the one villain that would derail him.

As we discover and unleash our influence, we become more aware of where insecurity is lurking. We recognize the places where it's hindering us, and we have a choice to either face our insecurity and deal with it or ignore the negative impact it will eventually have on our God-given influence.

INSECURITY IMPACTS OUR INFLUENCE

Insecurity doesn't go away on its own, and trying to ignore it does us no good. Moses gave an honest account of wrestling with doubts and insecurities when they intersect with the calling of God on one's life. I don't envy the task that Moses had in front of him—leading the Israelites out of Egypt and establishing their new nation. Beset by the challenges of leading a group of people who were uncooperative, doubted the vision, were disobedient, worshiped idols, and often criticized him, Moses had plenty of reason to doubt himself and God's calling.

When God told Moses that he was sending him to Pharaoh

to lead the Israelites out of Egypt, Moses responded, "Who am I that I should go to Pharaoh and bring the Israelites out of Egypt?" (Ex. 3:11). As they continued the conversation, Moses pressed God for reasons why the Israelites should follow his leading. Again, you sense his uncertainty. God responded with a powerful pep talk and informed Moses that he needed to tell the people, "The LORD, the God of your fathers—the God of Abraham, the God of Isaac and the God of Jacob—has sent me to you" (v. 15). But Moses fired back with more doubts: "What if they do not believe me or listen to me and say, 'The LORD did not appear to you'?" (4:1).

At this point, I'm pretty impressed by God's patience with Moses. Numerous times he reminded Moses that he had been called to lead the Israelites to the promised land. Wouldn't God's assurance be enough to instill confidence? But it didn't stop there. In response to Moses' question, God performed two miracles that Moses was to share as proof that God was with them. First, he turned Moses' walking stick into a serpent and instructed Moses to grab it by the tail. When he did, it turned back into his cane. Second, he afflicted Moses' hand with leprosy and healed it completely. God proceeded to tell Moses that if the people still wouldn't listen to him, Moses should take water from the river and pour it on the dry land, where it would become blood. With all these concrete assurances of God's guidance, one would think Moses' confidence would be growing.

And yet Moses dared to admit one more insecurity, perhaps his most sensitive insecurity: "Moses said to the LORD, 'Pardon your servant, Lord. I have never been eloquent, neither in the past nor since you have spoken to your servant. I am slow of speech and tongue'" (4:10). Another translation says that Moses exclaimed, "Oh, my Lord, I am not eloquent" (ESV). I can just hear the desperation and the self-doubt tormenting him. Even with all the promises that God made to be with him as he led the Israelites, insecurity still gnawed at him. Ultimately he begged God, "Please send someone else" (4:13).

It's tempting to look at that story and think, *Good grief, Moses, get it together.* Knowing what we know about how God used his influence, it seems ridiculous that Moses would wrestle with so many doubts and insecurities. And yet, this is exactly what we do with our insecurities. Much like Moses, we're blinded to our potential because we cannot see beyond our weakness.

We're blinded to our potential because we cannot see beyond our weakness.

Before we're too quick to criticize Moses, however, I do admire the fact that he was willing to admit his insecurities rather than cover them up and make himself look better than he actually felt. He was honest and vulnerable about the insecurities holding him back. His reaction is the opposite of what most of us are tempted to do.

CONFRONTING INSECURITY

How you respond to insecurity can drastically impact your influence. Tim's and Rebecca's stories from the beginning of the chapter portray the stark differences in the trajectory of our influence if we allow insecurity to gain a foothold. Author Beth Moore explained it well: "Not only will insecurity cheat us of reaching and then *operating consistently* at maximum potential, it also will turn our coworkers into threats and trap us into becoming posers."[4]

For leaders, insecurity can assume dangerous disguises. Often when we think of insecure people, mousy, timid, wallflower types come to mind. But that's not typically what insecurity looks like for leaders. Perhaps that is why we're so prone to ignore it; we don't always recognize it.

Some insecure leaders learn to mask their "I am not enough" fears with false confidence, gregariousness, brassiness, and bossiness. Other insecure leaders hide their lack of confidence behind performance. In their quest to be enough, they continue to focus on achievement, believing they can perform their way into the approval of others and ultimately into the self-confidence they seek.

That's how insecurity has played out for me. If I'm not enough, I will do everything I possibly can to be enough. I'll get good grades. I'll be a great employee. I'll dress well. I'll earn awards. I'll do it all to prove to myself and others that I am enough.

But that's the trouble with insecurity. It's never enough. Insecurity always sees what is missing about oneself.

You might be inclined to be insecure about the very thing that makes you unique. This is comparison creeping in again. I'm not the life of the party. I'm a more serious, contemplative type. At times I get really frustrated about this. I measure my weakness in this area by not getting invited to parties and missing out on social opportunities. I'm not sought out to share the latest office gossip. I'm not the first one on my friends' call lists when they need to be cheered up. For years I've wallowed in the insecurities that come with recognizing the things I'm not.

I might not be the life of the party, but I am the person to call when people need someone to help them solve problems. If they need a voice of counsel or they need someone to help them create a long-term plan, I'm their girl.

Insecurity tells us if we're not included all the time, we must not be enough. Insecurity screams that we have to be all things to all people at all times. We're not designed for that impossibility, which is a sure path to burnout when we give it a valiant try.

Insecurity can take on numerous faces and impact our influence in a variety of ways. As you read through these examples, look for hints of how insecurity might show up for you.

- *Insecure leaders become the influenced rather than the influencers.* Because they are so susceptible to others' impressions, they cater their actions and decisions to what will appease them. Rather than be confident in the perspective they bring, they temper their ideas and give only a fraction of their true selves. In turn, they rob themselves and others of their unique God-given influence.
- *Insecure leaders sometimes come across as aloof and insensitive.* In your insecurity you don't engage with others. Leaders who remain cold and distant from others have an air of superiority. You don't feel this way, of course; you feel the exact opposite. Yet because of your position of influence, people rarely assume that you lack confidence. They perceive that you just don't care.
- *Insecure leaders can assume an air of false confidence or pride.* They overcompensate for their insecurity by appearing to have limitless confidence. Boisterous, gregarious, opinionated, strong, and direct, an insecure

leader bullies his or her way into influence by being the most assertive person in the room.

- *Insecure leaders can be controlling and inflexible.* The only way they know to manage their world is by keeping tight control. They are terrified of change because it means confronting the unknown. Confronting the unknown could result in failure, and they perceive failure as the ultimate verdict that they are not enough.

- *Insecure leaders blame others when things don't go well.* They get angry because they see their team's failure as a poor reflection on themselves. While leaders are responsible for their teams, insecure leaders view team mistakes as personal defeat. They are more interested in defending themselves than having their team grow from the situation.

- *Insecure leaders find fault with everyone else.* They often hold themselves to a very high standard. In turn they have extraordinary and often unrealistic expectations of everyone else. If they can point out the weaknesses in others, they subconsciously see themselves as better.

- *Insecure leaders see themselves as victims.* Everyone else is the enemy. They are forever on the defensive and rarely able to believe the best in others.

- *Insecure leaders resist feedback.* They always have an excuse for why they do what they do. Because of their position, they have difficulty receiving feedback from people whom they don't perceive to have greater authority than they do. In other words, they don't seek to learn from everyone and every situation.

- *Insecure leaders measure everything against their internal structure of hierarchy.* They create a pecking order for everyone and are constantly measuring their position. Their goal is the top, and they are more focused on what it takes to get themselves there than to help everyone grow along the way.

- *Insecure leaders absorb the emotions of everyone around them.* When the team is discouraged, they are discouraged. When someone else is unhappy, they are unhappy. When their boss is cranky, they become uneasy because of her crankiness.
- *Insecure leaders can be obsessive people pleasers.* Fearful of losing favor, they waffle in making decisions that make others uncomfortable. As a result, their leadership is lackluster, void of the convictions that set leaders apart.

Where do you see yourself in these descriptions? Are you most consistently prone to two or three of them? We all will find ourselves there from time to time, but if many of them resonate regularly, let me encourage you to seriously confront the insecurities that are holding you back.

Insecurity has been the most distressing clout killer for me thus far. Every one of those examples has shown up in my life and some of them with embarrassing regularity. I once had someone very close to me say that he couldn't imagine what God would do through me if I could tackle this enemy of insecurity. What could God do through you if you confronted this hurdle of insecurity?

The most surprising thing I have learned about insecurity is that insecurity makes you selfish and self-focused. Ironically it is the opposite of what I thought I was. I thought I was being sensitive to the needs and perceptions of others, but I was only sensitive to others because of how it impacted me. If my boss didn't praise me for a project, I assumed that I must have done something wrong. Never mind that he might have a hundred other priorities that day. The fact that he didn't take the time to praise me must mean that I had done something wrong. If a friend didn't return my phone call, she must be upset with me. It couldn't be because she had an insanely busy day and didn't have a chance to call me back. Insecurity's goal is to keep us fixated on ourselves, wallowing in our "I am not enough" fears.

> *Having insecurity in your life is like having a wrecking ball constantly swinging through your soul.*

Having insecurity in your life is like having a wrecking ball constantly swinging through your soul. Hit after hit wears you down until you have nothing left to lead from. You're ashamed of its control in your life, but you feel powerless to stop its repeated hits. The constant destruction of your confidence leads to incredible self-doubt. Your fear of not being enough seems validated by the behaviors that insecurity brings out in you. Admitting to these insecure feelings seems so demeaning. You tell yourself that a good leader should be able to rise above them.

EXCHANGING INSECURITY FOR LOVE

What's the antidote? What's the replacement that combats insecurity in our lives? I believe the answer is found in Jesus' instruction to "love the Lord your God with all your heart and with all your soul and with all your mind" and "love your neighbor as yourself" (Matt. 22:37, 39). In other words, love God and love others. Insecurity must be countered with love. At its core, insecurity causes us to question our significance. We cannot love well when we're grappling for our self-worth. When we affirm the value of others by loving them well, our self-worth increases.

As it has been with each of our enemies, replacing insecurity is a journey that begins with a perspective change. To overcome insecurity we have to take the focus off ourselves and place it on others. That's the sneaky thing about insecurity. We believe we're not thinking about ourselves because we have such an unhealthy view of ourselves. But our fixation on our perceived inadequacies causes us to stay focused inward rather than outward. The more we remain focused on ourselves, the more we get sucked into the vortex of insecurity. If you've ever been in that place awhile, you understand the feeling that your insecurities are constantly trying to pull you under.

Perhaps because this one is so sensitive and personal to me I've been seeking a simple three-step plan that will be a miracle cure for your battle with insecurity. I'm going to give you a three-step plan, but I'll warn you that it's not a miracle cure. Rather, it's a guide to help you reframe your perspective.

1. IDENTIFY WHERE INSECURITY IS IMPACTING YOUR INFLUENCE

Acknowledge the ways that you're susceptible to feelings of self-doubt. Perhaps you can share this with a trusted friend or family member and ask for help to be more aware of when insecurity is getting the best of you.

When I see the signs of insecurity popping up, I take a few

minutes and write about it in a journal. I document the feelings of insecurity and try to discern what about the situation is causing them. Doing this keeps me from sinking deeper into my feelings of insecurity because I'm acknowledging them head-on rather than ignoring them. It helps me see patterns in how insecurity impacts me, and it also helps me identify victories as I look back through my journals and recognize ways that I've grown.

2. Commit It to Prayer

I'll assume the risk of this sounding like a Sunday school answer because for as much as we know this, we don't do it: "[Cast] all your care upon Him, for He cares for you" (1 Peter 5:7 NKJV). What if we really embraced the idea that God cares deeply about the things that concern us? And what's more, he cares deeply about the things that are holding us back from doing the creative best with the life he has given each of us to live.

I believe this is where Moses got it right. Rather than cover up or mask his insecurities, he brazenly took them to God. The Bible tells us that God got angry with him at one point (Ex. 4:14). But once Moses confronted his insecurities by taking them to God and allowing God to reframe his perspective, Moses' leadership flourished.

3. Turn Your Attention to Others

When you're tempted to be insecure, look for something you can do for someone else. Find anything. Interrupt your inner dialogue, and do something for someone else. When you're feeling insignificant, how can you make someone else feel special? If you are feeling like a failure, how can you encourage someone else? If you're fearful of losing influence, how can you champion someone else?

It's not about you; it's about Christ in you. Insecurity makes it all about me. *Did I do enough? Was I good enough? Am I smart enough?* The replacement perspective is that it's not about you but about what God can do through you. Your self-worth is no longer on the line when this perspective shifts.

As with every enemy we've been discussing, insecurity is another attempt to inhibit our God-given influence. Overcoming it starts with teaching ourselves the habit of identifying when this clout killer is lurking and replacing it with an intentional choice to take the focus off ourselves and direct it toward loving and encouraging others.

DISCOVERY STEPS

- What part of the definition of *insecurity* most resonates with you? Can you identify where this insecurity may have started?
- Where do you see insecurity impacting your influence? Which of the examples from pages 71–73 can you relate to?
- What steps can you take to identify insecurity more quickly in your life and take it to God?
- Look for situations in which you can turn insecurities into opportunities to love and encourage others.

CHAPTER 6

YOU DON'T HAVE TO KNOW IT ALL

Purging Pride

If you are humble, nothing will touch you, neither praise nor disgrace, because you know what you are.

—MOTHER TERESA[1]

WE HAD REACHED A STALEMATE. AS I LOOKED around the room at my team, I was staring into the faces of incredibly strong-willed and passionate individuals who were not going to budge on their opinion. I was convinced they were wrong. They were convinced they were right. Everything in me wanted to play the trump card: I was the boss. I could settle this. With one statement I could make the decision and move us along. But in a rare moment of maturity I knew that my pride just wanted to win. I was resistant to their concerns because I thought I knew better. I had more experience. I had more historical context for the situation.

We were in a battle of wills, a battle of pride. And neither side was willing to give in. With every concern they raised, I had a quick retort. With every question they asked, I had a solid answer. The more they pushed, the more I pushed back. The longer the conversation continued, the more stubborn we became about our positions for the argument. We weren't going to get anywhere until we were willing to let go of our pride and humbly listen to one another.

Pride doesn't show up one day and overtake us with excessive force. Pride infuses our thoughts and grows as it is given space. We don't aspire to it, and we don't believe we've become victims of it until it has inflicted damage that requires significant amounts of repair. We often describe it as passion, perhaps even conviction, therefore deceiving ourselves about how it wars within us.

Pride is like a facade on the exterior of our souls. We use it in the attempt to disguise our other clout killers. While our fears and insecurities cover us layer upon layer, pride quickly responds with a false exterior to tidy it all up.

> *Pride fools others and us into believing that we've got it all together.*

Pride fools others and us into believing that we've got it all together. We become unrecognizable to ourselves. We're rarely aware that we've built this facade, which makes it all the more difficult for us to identify when pride is impacting our influence.

Here's another way to think about it: If I am a car driving down the road of life, fears, insecurities, and comparisons are the obstacles that can often give me a flat tire. When these enemies force me off the road, I may respond by putting on the spare tire of pride. It's a quick repair that keeps me moving. But while I may be able to keep going with the spare tire of pride, I know I am limited. I can't go quite as fast or as far. I'm more tentative. I have to play it safe. I intend to get a replacement, but sometimes I get so busy I don't take time to replace pride with the real thing. I become used to it. I'm comfortable. I'm too busy to pay attention to the temporary fix that I've created. The longer I drive with the limits of this feeble cover-up, the more damage I inflict on other parts of myself.

As I stared around the room at the faces of my team, my inner dialogue was trying to discern where pride was speaking. *Are my convictions authentic, or are they a reaction to the layers of my prideful facade? Do I just want to be right because my insecurities can't handle being wrong? Do I think I should have the right answer because my fears convince me that having the wrong one would indicate I am not a good leader? Do I need to be right because comparison tells me that to be right makes me better than the others?*

When we haven't done the work of discovering our God-given influence, we build a false identity. Unknowingly we allow the clout killers to influence every situation. Without truth, we build upon lies. Our ego—our pride—is warring within us to build something different from who we truly are. If, much like me, you didn't know to make a careful exploration early in your life, you've spent years building a false self.

Pride by definition is "inordinate self-esteem"[2] or, said another way, excessive confidence in oneself. Honestly, I don't buy that definition. I think pride is the *illusion* of excessive self-esteem. Most people whom we perceive as prideful are actually doing everything they can to convince others that they have confidence in themselves. I have yet to meet someone who is truly prideful without his pride being triggered by the core fear that continuously impacts clout—the "I am not enough" fear. Pride causes us to overcompensate for this base fear. What we say, what we do, and how we lead stem from our efforts to appear more confident than we really are.

Many of our lives look like this. We've built so many layers that it's nearly impossible for anyone—even us—to know what our true God-given influence looks like. We're proud of the false exterior and the distractions we've created. Perhaps we built them out of one of our fears: the fear that I'm not enough so I'll build something that looks better, or the fear that I don't have enough so I'll keep adding layers. Once again pride confronts us with our "I am not enough" fears.

Pride Impacts Our Influence

The apostle Peter was a leader who displayed inordinate self-esteem. Regarded as the first disciple whom Jesus named, as well as one of the three disciples to be a part of Jesus' inner circle, Peter likely found a great deal of pride in his position. Peter is a picture-perfect case of how our underlying fears motivate our pride. In three specific instances, we can see symptoms of pride in Peter's life:

Overconfidence

When Jesus walked on water toward the disciples in the boat, Peter tested him with the challenge, "Lord, if it's you, tell me to come to you on the water." Jesus said, "Come," and I imagine Peter stepped out with a "look at me" swagger. But as quickly as his arrogance emerged, fear responded, and Peter exclaimed, "Lord, save me!" (Matt. 14:28–30).

DESPERATION

During those intense few moments in the Garden of Gethsemane when Judas led the soldiers to arrest Jesus, I imagine that once again fear gripped Peter. Perhaps he felt remorse or guilt for repeatedly falling asleep when he was supposed to be keeping watch as Jesus prayed. In a desperate move to protect Jesus and prove his worth, Peter impulsively lopped off the ear of one soldier, leaving Jesus to apologize and clean up the mess.

DENIAL

Unfortunately Peter's greatest legacy may be fulfilling Jesus' prediction that Peter would deny him three times before the rooster crowed. Despite vehemently promising that he would not deny Jesus, Peter did exactly what Jesus said he would do. When the heat of the moment tested Peter's character, his weakness won out.

Pride drives us to behave in ways that aren't true to the core of our character. It's as if pride's personality takes over our own. Rather than address the fears and insecurities underlying pride, we overcompensate. Like Peter, we become overconfident in our attitudes and responses in order to

> *Pride drives us to behave in ways that aren't true to the core of our character.*

prove to ourselves and others that we're not afraid. Pushed to the limit, we'll act out of desperation and impulsively do things inconsistent with our clout. Backed into a corner, we'll respond with denial.

For a leader, this more specifically looks like the following:

- *Overcompensating.* You boldly proceed with an initiative even though others have tentatively raised concerns. Your fear of not looking as if you know what you're doing drives you to overcompensate with aggressive action.
- *Impulsiveness.* You make impulsive decisions because you don't want to hear concerns from others. Your ego can't handle their catching something that you didn't.
- *Excuse making.* You always have excuses when things don't go as well as you planned. You always pin the blame on someone or something else, and you deny any fault on your part.
- *Resistance.* You become belligerent, digging in your heels and resisting feedback from others. You avoid engaging people or circumstances that challenge your opinions.
- *Unteachability.* You are convinced that your way is the best way, and you can't find value in others' opinions.
- *Defiance.* You are defiant and boldly argue with others, even with those in authority over you.
- *Blindness.* You are so focused on proving yourself that you are blinded to other sides of the issue.

In a *Fast Company* article, Ken and Scott Blanchard described the effects of pride this way: "When people get caught up in their egos, it erodes their effectiveness. That's because the combination of false pride and self-doubt created by an overactive ego gives people a distorted image of their own importance.

When that happens, people see themselves as the center of the universe and they begin to put their own agenda, safety, status, and gratification ahead of those affected by their thoughts and actions."[3]

During numerous seasons of my leadership, many of these prideful traits have shown up, but many of them were evident at the same time in one season, and it was not my finest hour.

I was just hitting my stride in my career in the music business. I felt capable and confident. I had earned influence and a reasonable level of authority. I was favored, and I knew it. Then seemingly out of nowhere our company went through a corporate merger in which I found myself on the outside of the "in" crowd. I was frustrated by the lack of respect I felt through the process, and I quite arrogantly believed that I was not given what I deserved. Convinced I was more competent than my new bosses and peers, I set out to prove them wrong for positioning me so poorly. I was defiant, uncooperative, resistant, and unteachable. I was disrespectful to my leaders and unkind to my coworkers.

I'm terribly embarrassed by the memory of my behavior, but back then I was blinded by the fears and insecurities that pride was painfully overcompensating for. If someone had confronted me about my pride, I likely would have lashed out with all the excuses for why I had been mistreated and disrespected. I believed it wasn't me; it was them.

In my pride, I was unwilling to listen. I was deafened to the signs of my character that were contrary to who I really wanted to be. I was resistant to the coaching of mentors who assured me that if I was patient, more opportunities would develop. I was defiant and unteachable because I thought I was right. And I was quick to make excuses for my bad attitude. Pride opened the door for the other clout killers to show up too. Jealous of others' opportunities, I criticized them rather than celebrated them. Insecure about my influence, I controlled and blamed others rather than loving and supporting them. Operating out of scarcity, I protected and defended my territory rather than generously investing in others.

When we recognize these symptoms of pride in our lives, we have to pause to listen. Unwillingness to listen is a sure sign that pride is inching its way into our hearts. It's evidence that we're building a false exterior. We're unwilling to listen because of the fear of what we might discover.

Confronting Pride

No one aspires to pride. We don't actively set out to be resistant to feedback or insensitive to others. It isn't pride that we want. It's the desires that pride falsely fulfills. Our desire is to discover our clout. We want to unleash our God-given influence. But pride falsely feeds this deep-seated longing, seducing us into becoming satisfied with a shallow imitation of the influence we desperately desire.

Perfection

Pride feeds our longing for perfection. It's a quest for competency. We want to be the best. We want to give our best. Pride says that you must prove your worth and perform your way to acceptance. Pride finds all its value and worth in your accomplishments and sends you spinning emotionally out of control when you don't measure up to the expectations you have created for yourself. Pride finds its value in what you do rather than in who God says you are. Pride can't be comfortable with imperfection.

Sarah Young wrote in the devotional *Jesus Calling*, "Thinking that you should live an error-free life is symptomatic of pride. Your failures can be a source of blessing, humbling you and giving you empathy for other people in their weaknesses."[4]

Pride is at work in our lives when we're unwilling to admit what we don't know and to define our inadequacies. Pride keeps us from being dependent on God. It shortchanges our clout because it holds us back from exploring the areas that can't be controlled. Pride shifts our reliance on God to reliance on ourselves.

> *Pride falsely feeds this deep-seated longing, seducing us into becoming satisfied with a shallow imitation of the influence we desperately desire.*

IMPORTANCE

Pride convinces us that we're more important than anyone else. *My schedule is more important. My time is more valuable.* Pride takes its cues from our other enemies and keeps building upon them:

- Insecurity triggers our awareness of hierarchy. *If I'm at or near the top of the ladder, I must be more important.*
- Comparison adds to the argument. *My gifts have gotten me to where I am, so they must be more valuable than someone else's.*
- And fear perpetuates the cycle. *I must cling to these things in which I've found my value, or I won't be enough.*

Pride allows us to believe that our leadership and influence are more important than the gifts and influence of others.

This can be incredibly deceptive, especially for those of us who have positions of influence. Pride will convince us that because we have more responsibility and greater accountability, our gifts make us better or more important than others. Although our gifts may make us different and they may require more in some areas, they do not make us more important.

In his book *Love Works*, Joel Manby tells the story of Judy, an employee at one of the fourteen locations that Joel leads as president and CEO of Herschend Family Entertainment: "No one at Dollywood has a greater impact on the organizational culture than Judy." He goes on to say, "Dollywood literally wouldn't be the extremely friendly, successful family entertainment park that it is today without Judy."[5] While Judy is an executive assistant by title, Joel clarifies, "Judy is as 'senior' as anyone from an influence standpoint."[6] (Joel got America's attention when his countercultural methods of leadership were put to the test on an episode of the CBS hit reality show *Undercover Boss*.) Convinced that "leading with love" is the way of wise managers,[7] Joel redefined what builds an organizational hierarchy and confirmed that humility establishes one's value and importance.

PERFORMANCE

Pride finds tremendous value in performance because it can be measured. We can see how we're doing in relation to others. Performance becomes a measurement for comparison. We compare our performance by keeping track of all our accomplishments—awards, grades, sports, spouse, kids, job, salary, house, cars, and friends. The more we have, the better we must be.

Additionally pride tempts us to believe that we're managing our gifts better than others do. This is a big one for me. My history has given me many reasons not to succeed, but I have worked incredibly hard to overcome them. I've been diligent and focused. I've been purposeful and successful. And I've become proud of myself for that.

If I'm honest, I often believe that others just haven't worked hard enough; anyone can make something of himself if he just applies himself. I subconsciously believe if I can do it, anyone can, and I actually become annoyed at someone who squanders her gifts. Even though all those things might be true, that thought process is pride. It's not my job to compare, criticize, or judge others. My job is to discover and unleash my God-given influence and be faithful to lead from this position.

INDEPENDENCE

Pride deceives us into thinking that we can handle it all on our own. A sense of power comes with independence. When I'm independent I don't need others. I don't have to wait on others. I can move faster. I can do more.

Assured that you can do it better by yourself, you resist help or support. Other times you may be afraid of admitting that you don't know what you're doing. Rather than ask for help, you power through on your own. When you accomplish a task, you don't ask for feedback for fear that you won't like what you'll hear.

Independence leads us to falsely believe that we are better by ourselves. But in 2 Corinthians 3:5 the apostle Paul reminded us, "Not that we are competent in ourselves to claim anything for ourselves, but our competence comes from God." We are not designed to be independent. We are created to be dependent on God and to live in community with others.

EXCHANGING PRIDE FOR HUMILITY

Personally I think Peter gets a bad rap. Many of us are too quick to judge Peter, who is famously remembered for denying Jesus three times. Our self-righteousness gets the better of us, and whether we admit it or not, we're tempted to believe that in his shoes, we never would have denied Jesus. Jesus predicted that Peter would deny him three times, but Jesus previously made another very powerful prediction. He said that Peter (whose name means "rock") would be the rock upon which Christ's church would be built (Matt. 16:18). Both of Jesus' predictions came true, and I believe one made way for the other.

> *The desire to wholeheartedly follow God was at war with prideful longings for perfection, importance, performance, and independence.*

Peter's greater legacy—his clout—is that he did indeed become instrumental in developing the early church. In his early years, Peter's pride walked hand in hand with his faith. The desire to wholeheartedly follow God was at war with prideful longings for perfection, importance, performance, and independence. His faith and his failure coexisted. Isn't that how it is for most of us?

When the rooster crowed, the trajectory of Peter's influence was radically altered. He immediately remembered Jesus' words, and Scripture tells us he "wept bitterly" (Matt. 26:75).

I'm picturing a heartbreaking, gut-wrenching, fall-to-his-knees cry. Peter was broken. God had gotten his attention, and he recognized how significantly pride had impacted his influence and broken the heart of Christ. At that moment, I believe Peter made his replacement. He exchanged pride for humility, and after that, his influence flourished.

I see Peter's face when I read this description from Parker Palmer: "The path to humility, for some of us at least, goes through humiliation, where we are brought low, rendered powerless, stripped of pretenses and defenses, and left feeling fraudulent, empty, and useless—a humiliation that allows us to regrow our lives from the ground up, from the humus of common ground."[8]

Has the rooster crowed in your life? Have you encountered a season that humbled you so deeply that you recognized your need to permanently replace pride with a heart of humility?

Proverbs 11:2 speaks of the effects of pride and humility: "When pride comes, then comes disgrace, / but with humility comes wisdom." Too many leaders have been marked by disgrace. Even if they were able to replace their pride and move forward with humility, such as Peter did, their legacies still tell the story of pride.

To avoid the rooster of disgrace, we must continually look for ways to replace pride with humility. That exploration begins with honesty and community.

HONESTY

We must be honest about pride's impact on our influence. Where might you be acting overconfidently or impulsively? What are you in denial about? Humility begins with being honest with yourself. Pastor Rick Warren explained, "The better [you] know yourself, the less prideful you'll be. Honesty creates humility. Self-deception leads to self-destruction."[9] Like Peter, are you deceiving yourself in any area of your life? Are you pursuing perfection? Are you longing for importance? Are you performing your way to significance, or are you relying on your independence?

Until you are willing to be honest about the corners where pride is lurking, you'll be ignorant of the warning signs.

COMMUNITY

When you're operating from a place of pride, everyone knows it but you.

A humble heart opens itself up; a prideful heart stays closed and protective. A humble heart listens to others; a prideful heart resists feedback. A humble heart asks questions; a prideful heart moves forward independently. A humble heart seeks out others; a prideful heart keeps its distance.

Humility allows you to surround yourself with people smarter than you. Pride holds you back and inhibits you from vulnerably acknowledging you don't know something.

Humility embraces community for the value of collective wisdom. Pride resists community because it's threatened by sharing ideas and successes with others, leaving you isolated and alone.

Humility changes your paradigm from *I* to *we*. Humility is thinking about yourself less and thinking about others more. In humility you begin to recognize the value of others. You're less afraid to be open about the enemies pride previously tempted you to cover up. You're honest about where fear, insecurity, scarcity, and comparison impact you. In this place of vulnerability you find community and discover that you are more accepted for being who you are than for the false exterior you've projected.

Humble Confidence

Out of Peter's brokenness emerged humble confidence. Humble confidence is the outcome of careful exploration. Where pride finds its identity in perfection, importance, performance, and independence, humility allows us to anchor our identity in Christ first and live from a place of confidence in Christ in us. This was true for Peter, and the same can be true for each of us:

- Where pride was once rooted in arrogance, your confidence becomes rooted in Christ.
- Where pride says you have to prove your worth, confidence says God has determined your worth.
- Where pride takes credit for your accomplishments, confidence humbly acknowledges God's work in you.

This replacement doesn't come easily, but it is possible. When a leader chooses the path of humility, he impacts the entire culture of the team or organization. Doug Guthrie and Sudhir Venkatesh wrote about this in a *Forbes* article: "Individuals who know themselves are courageously

Humility allows us to anchor our identity in Christ first and live from a place of confidence in Christ in us.

able to pursue creative leadership. What is profoundly powerful about embracing humility and publicly acknowledging errors is the link between authenticity and the success of the individual and the organization."[10]

Remember the stalemate with my team from the beginning of the chapter? All it took was one team member who chose to humble himself and admit that his opinion might not be right, and the entire tone of the conversation changed. Because he was willing to lead with humility, we all let our guards down and chose to open ourselves to the various possibilities. We concluded that meeting with a unified decision and, more important, a stronger sense of camaraderie.

I suspect that the majority of us have to be tripped up by pride a time or two before we understand how significantly pride has been impacting our lives. When we acknowledge our attempts to create the illusion of excessive self-esteem and recognize the fears that trigger our attempts to create this false facade, we allow humble confidence to make way for our God-given influence to thrive.

DISCOVERY STEPS

- What enemy (or enemies) is pride trying to cover up in your life: fear, comparison, jealousy, scarcity, envy, or insecurity?
- What desire is pride falsely fulfilling for you: perfection, importance, performance, or independence?
- Where do you need to get truly honest about pride's impact on your life?
- Where can you invite community in to make the replacement for humility?

CHAPTER 7

YOU CAN LET GO

Relinquishing Control

It seems easier to be God than to love God, easier to control people than to love people.

—HENRI NOUWEN[1]

UPON MY FIRST VISIT TO LONDON, ENGLAND, I had one key destination in mind: the Tower of London, the ominous stone-walled fortress that served as the symbol of power for the English monarchy for hundreds of years. I arrived that early September morning amid a cloud of London fog as it rolled in off the River Thames. The eerie scene of the great tower emerging through the ghostly atmosphere foreshadowed the stories I heard once I passed through the very same gates that made way for the likes of William the Conqueror and Henry VIII.

I've been fascinated by royalty as long as I can remember. I love the pomp and circumstance and pageantry. I love the grandeur, the spectacle, and the significance that accompany the elites. I'm intrigued by the air of privilege and the opulence with which they live. But if I'm honest, I'm most intrigued by their power. As I wandered the grounds and absorbed the stories of the characters who gave the tower its numerous faces—a citadel of defense, a palace for dignitaries, a prison of state, an armory for war, and a treasury for the crown jewels—I was torn between the prestige of power and the destruction originated within those walls. So many of those leaders had absolute rule, and unfortunately history is filled with their horror stories.

The historian and moralist known as Lord Acton is credited with saying, "Power tends to corrupt and absolute power corrupts absolutely. Great men are almost always bad men."[2] The "great men" Lord Acton referred to are those in positions of power. He was talking about leaders. What a despairing viewpoint of something that was intended to be a God-given gift. Why is it common for those who are given power to succumb to corruption? Is it possible for leaders to have influence without yielding to the ills of control? Can we lead and motivate others without relenting to the seduction of power?

Control is simply a need for power, but as if the definition of control was not enough, the phrase "control freak" has earned its own definition: "a person whose behavior indicates a powerful need to control people or circumstances in everyday matters."[3] Control freaks grasp for power. Some find that power in controlling people. Others find it in controlling circumstances, and still others find power in controlling both. The problem with power is that it is an insatiable need. There is always more power to gain and more territory to conquer. In his book *The Control Freak*, psychologist Les Parrott defined *control freaks* as "people who care more than you do about something and won't stop at being pushy to get their way."[4]

A longing for power—a desire for control—is an indicator that we're not content with the influence we've been given. It's a sign that we're trying to manufacture influence we don't have. We're seeking significance from a source that won't satiate. In attempting to control what we can't, we neglect what we can. By choosing control, we neglect to operate from the clout we have been given.

Control is the dark side of influence. What may start as an innocent desire to lead and motivate others can quickly turn into a deep need to control and manipulate. Power feeds insecurity's need for a sense of social order. We feel the need to position ourselves above others to feed our desire to be valued. Control is a distortion of influ-

> *A longing for power—a desire for control—is an indicator that we're not content with the influence we've been given.*

ence. Where influence guides and motivates others, control directs and manipulates others. True influence doesn't seek power. Control can't live without it.

Control can be glaringly obvious or deceptively subtle. It's glaringly obvious in stories of the tyrants of history, such as Herod the Great, Adolf Hitler, and Saddam Hussein. It's obvious in the actions of a highly dictatorial boss or an obsessive-compulsive spouse. But control is deceptively subtle when we look in the mirror. We have trouble seeing control in ourselves because it's another unattractive clout killer.

In a critical growth season of my leadership, my organization hired a consultant to conduct a 360-degree review of my leadership. This popular form of performance assessment measures your effectiveness not just by your boss's perceptions but also by the opinions and feedback of your peers and your employees. The results were painful and, unfortunately for me, accurate. Several coworkers and staff members felt that I had a tendency to control too many details. They felt micromanaged and not trusted. As a result they were demotivated and sometimes resentful. I was taken aback by their feedback. I did not perceive myself as controlling. I considered myself thorough. I felt responsible for the outcomes, and I managed accordingly.

I didn't realize that control was just another by-product of many of my other enemies. Fear was once again at the root, and my influence was being inhibited.

A *Psychology Today* article described the relationship between fear and control: "One of the most prevalent fears people have is that of losing control. This is the fear that if you don't manage to control the outcome of future events, something terrible will happen."[5] I was petrified of losing control. I was afraid that if I didn't tightly manage my team, I would lose all control of the outcomes. My "I am not enough" fear came screaming to the surface again.

Fear of what you can't control will only keep you from doing what you can.

Fear of what you can't control will only keep you from doing what you can. When fear is driving your need for control, you slowly squeeze the life out of the people around you. You become intense and unfriendly. You are never satisfied. You demotivate your team and inhibit their gifts from flourishing. You create a tone of tension in your work environments and instill fear in everyone else. That was exactly what I was doing, yet I was sadly unaware of how controlling I was. By defining my actions as being thorough and responsible, I was feeding myself the illusion of competence. I wasn't competent. I was controlling.

CONTROL IMPACTS OUR INFLUENCE

Most of us come by our control issues honestly. Our driving motivation is to do great. To lead well. To handle our influence responsibly. Moses is one of my favorite examples of this motivation in action.

In Exodus 18, Moses was reestablishing some order for the Israelites. God had recently given them victory over the Amalekites, and they were experiencing freedom once again. Moses had just come through an extraordinarily trying time as a leader, but things were looking up. He was eager to establish normalcy and routine. In fact, he received word that his father-in-law, Jethro, would be coming to see him and bringing Moses' wife and children back to him after being sent away during battle.

Once Jethro arrived he expressed delight over what God had done for Moses and the Israelites, and they celebrated together by offering a sacrifice to God. The next day, Moses went back to work, and Jethro accompanied him. I suspect that Moses had a spring in his step. God's people were free, Moses' family was reunited, and he was back to work acting as judge for the Israelite people. All day long, from morning until night, he settled disputes.

Likely eager for approval and affirmation, Moses must have been caught off guard by Jethro's feedback: "What is this you are doing for the people? Why do you alone sit as judge, while all these people stand around you from morning till evening?" (Ex. 18:14). Moses responded with a rational excuse, "Because the people come to me to seek God's will" (v. 15). Imagine how dev-astated he must have felt when Jethro flatly stated, "What you are doing is not good. You and these people who come to you will only wear yourselves out. The work is too heavy for you; you can-not handle it alone" (vv. 17–18).

Moses must have been completely deflated by that point. Moses' intentions were good. He wanted to lead the Israelites well. He was eager to help them get their lives on track. But perhaps out of his fear of failure or maybe his insecurity in leading them well, he chose to handle everything by himself. He chose to keep all the con-trol and, as a result, was on a path to exhaustion and ineffectiveness.

I don't think Moses had a malicious desire to control every-thing. I think he truly wanted the best for God's people, but his position of influence opened the door for power and control that he couldn't identify in himself. Fortunately for Moses, someone he trusted and respected was bold enough to speak into his life before it was too late. And to Moses' credit, he was wise enough to listen.

Control can impact our influence in various ways, but we often see it in partnership with the other clout killers:

- *Insecurity* says you are not good enough, and in an attempt to prove you can handle it, you control.
- *Scarcity* suggests that there is not enough power to go around, so you control your territory by edging others out.
- *Comparison* causes you to try to control your circumstances so that you can keep pace with others.
- *Pride* motivates you to try to prove your value by being the one to direct all the answers.

- *Fear* says you cannot fail, so you must control everything and everyone.

Les Parrott III summarized it this way: "The strain of constantly trying to keep from failing pushes them [control freaks] more and more into trying to control everything and everybody."[6] All our controlling tendencies boil down to two distinct things that we attempt to control—outcomes and others.

1. Outcomes

My pastor and leader, Pete Wilson, says, "The greatest of illusions is control." Let's be honest. We don't really control anything. We can't control whether the sun rises or sets. We can't control who loves us. We can't control when we take our last breath. And yet we do everything we can to control our circumstances to manage around our fears. Fear of the unknown, fear of the what-ifs, and fear of "I am not enough" drive us to control as much of our worlds as we possibly can.

When we attempt to control outcomes, we might

- arrange our lives so as not to fail, either by avoiding circumstances that require risk or by managing the details of a situation so tightly that failure is edged out.
- chart such a distinct path for our lives that we are unwilling to bend or change our plans. In our inflexibility we miss out on new opportunities.
- manage our schedules so precisely that we leave no room for the unexpected. Fearful of surprises, we schedule every minute in an attempt to avoid uncertainty.

2. OTHERS

Because we can't do life without others, controllers quickly learn how to make others work for them. Even the outcomes we attempt to control are rarely accomplished without also controlling others in the process. Controlling people create an atmosphere where others are hypersensitive to how they'll react. They are never sure when they might step on a land mine.

When we attempt to control others, we might

- be superstrict parents. We may explain it as wanting the best for our children, but more often we're controlling how their behavior impacts the way in which others perceive us.
- be micromanagers in the workplace. There are seasons when highly directed work is necessary because of experience or circumstance, but when leaders micromanage every person and every situation, it's not about what's best for their employees or organization. They are doing what makes them feel powerful.
- be disrespectful spouses. Control in marriage looks like accountability without respect. It's demanding things from your spouse so that you know his or her every move and action, absent of trust.

CONFRONTING CONTROL

Sometimes our control of outcomes or others isn't driven from a direct need for power. It can also be birthed from a desire for perfection. Our intention to have everything perfectly ordered and structured manifests itself in controlling ways. We explain it as a desire for perfection, but it's really fed by a spirit of control or power. Brené Brown offered more insight on this dynamic:

> Wherever perfectionism is driving, shame is riding shotgun. Perfectionism is not about healthy striving, which you see all the time in successful leaders, it's not about trying to set goals and being the best we can be, perfectionism is basically a cognitive behavioral process that says if I look perfect, work perfect, and do everything perfectly, I can avoid shame, ridicule, and criticism. It's a defense mechanism.[7]

Our desire for control, whether intentional or not, becomes a burden of anxiety for us to carry. When our control is limited, our anxiety grows even greater. Writing in *Psychology Today*, Elliot Cohen elaborates further: "The crux of the problem is the demand for certainty in a world that is always tentative and uncertain. It is precisely this unrealistic demand that creates the anxiety. You think that you *must* accurately predict and manage the future, not just have some probabilistic and uncertain handle on it."[8]

Cross Point was in the middle of a huge initiative. Because the project was outside the scope of my usual responsibilities and experience, we hired an outside consultant to navigate it for us. This project was a major milestone in the life of our organization, and while I was not versed in the specifics, I was tasked with overseeing its completion. As things progressed and I became more entrenched in the details, I became anxiously aware of how much I didn't know about how to lead through it. After a few missed deadlines and communication challenges between the consultant and me, I became extraordinarily anxious about how we were going to complete the assignment. As my anxiety grew, my control increased. The only way I knew to attempt to diffuse my fears was to immerse myself in the details and take control of it.

Parts of our driven nature are natural by-products of our leadership gifts. We have what author and pastor Bill Hybels refers to as a "holy discontent." A holy discontent is the cause, problem, or issue that we have identified and can't help but do something about. Hybels wrote, "It is often these 'firestorms of frustration' that God will use to enlist you in setting what is wrong in this world right!"[9] Part of understanding our clout is identifying what makes us discontent. Our discontentment motivates us to see a future to which we are called to lead others. But our driven tendencies cross the line to control when our anxiety begins to take responsibility for the outcomes and the actions of others. That was where I was headed.

> *Our driven tendencies cross the line to control when our anxiety begins to take responsibility for the outcomes and the actions of others.*

Determined to figure out how to lead through the situation without resorting to my controlling tendencies, I evaluated the tension between control and trust. It was another replacement that I needed to embrace if I was willing to grow as a leader.

When we wrestle with a tendency to control, we have to position ourselves to trust first. When a large project or challenge is looming, my nature is to run to organize and structure it—to essentially create the illusion of control.

The better way to wrestle with this tension is to first take it to God in prayer and trust that he will provide the direction that we need. It's choosing to release control to him and then using the gifts he's given us to intentionally work through the challenge.

I used to think that trusting meant abdicating my responsibility, but I really believe trusting means choosing God first and in faith believing that he is ultimately in control. My control issues forced me to confront my propensity to ignore my dependency on God. Control feeds my independence and develops a false sense of personal responsibility. Leadership expert John Maxwell wisely explained: "Successful leaders . . . know the difference

I believe God does his greatest work through us when we are aware of our limitations and have to trust and lean into him for outcomes that are too big for us to tackle on our own.

between being in charge and being in control. We kid ourselves if we think we are in control. We may have charge of a group, but the best we can do is remain *under* control. God is the Ultimate Leader, and He is forever *in* control."[10]

The project that I was overseeing at Cross Point was perhaps the biggest challenge my leadership has faced thus far. Utterly beyond my capacity I came face-to-face with my limitations. Fortunately, much like Moses, I had wise leaders around me who were willing to confront my attempts to control.

The most dangerous place for us to be is in a situation where we feel that we've got it all under control in our own abilities. I believe God does his greatest work through us when we are aware of our limitations and have to trust and lean into him for outcomes that are too big for us to tackle on our own.

EXCHANGING CONTROL
FOR TRUST AND FAITH

The irony of our control issues is that the power we seek in our controlling tendencies is actually realized when we discover the power of God's work through us as we place our trust and faith in his ability rather than our own.

So how do you effectively replace control with trust and faith?

First, acknowledge your dependence on God. Recognize that you are not intended to handle life on your own, and you cannot do it on your own. Remember that you are just a steward. You are responsible only to be faithful. God is responsible for outcomes.

Second, accept your limitations. Take off the cape. You are not designed to be a superhero. Your limitations are reminders to own what you can and release control of what you can't. You must learn to manage the tension of being responsible for what you can but being dependent enough to know that God works through you to accomplish it all.

Third, embrace the opportunity to work with others. Being the leader doesn't mean that you have to direct every idea or decision. When you control, you limit the power that comes from a team working effectively together. When you control, you take the role of the dictator. Everyone else becomes your subject and either submits or revolts. As a leader, you release control in exchange for a spirit of partnership.

When you replace your controlling nature for trust and faith in God, you receive replacements for the issues that control triggered in your life.

ANXIETY FOR PEACE

In exchange for anxiety, we begin to experience peace. Philippians 4:6–7 states this clearly: "Do not be anxious about anything, but in every situation, by prayer and petition, with thanksgiving, present your requests to God. And the peace of God, which transcends all understanding, will guard your hearts and your minds in Christ Jesus."

COMPULSIVENESS FOR PATIENCE

In exchange for our intense and driven nature we can experience patience. Colossians 1:10–11 reminds us, "You may live a life worthy of the Lord and please him in every way: bearing fruit in every good work, growing in the knowledge of God, being strengthened with all power according to his glorious might so that you may have great endurance and patience."

Our attempts to control are rarely born from malicious intent. We long for power for the purpose of accomplishing what we're passionate about. Most good leaders are tempted to control, but great leaders learn how to control their controlling nature. Leaders who overcome the clout killer of control create cultures where peace and patience are prevalent. They foster confidence and competence rather than anxiety and frenzy. When leaders display not only trust in God but also trust in their team, they inspire faith.

I believe it is possible for us as leaders to be truly great men and women when we exchange the longing for power and control for the trust and faith that come from living in obedience to God. That's what discovering our clout is all about. As we make these replacements, we begin to see our leadership reflect the character and confidence of our God-given influence.

DISCOVERY STEPS

- Where do you see control impacting your influence?
- Are you most tempted to control outcomes or others or both?
- What are you anxious about? Is control driving your anxiety?
- What can you do to replace control with trust?

PART 2

THE 4 CLOUT CULTIVATORS

Identity
Confidence
Mission
Passion

CHAPTER 8

DISCOVERING YOUR IDENTITY

The drive to significance is a simple extension of the creative impulse of God. . . . It is outwardly directed to the good to be done. We were built to count, as water is made to run downhill. We are placed in a specific context to count in ways no one else does. That is our destiny.

—DALLAS WILLARD[1]

BY ALL APPEARANCES JOHN WAS NOT DESTINED for a life of significance. Brash, abrasive, aloof, aggressive, hostile, and nomadic, he was isolated and indifferent. Lacking a sense of purpose and meaning, John left a trail of broken relationships and broken promises. In his later years, John reflected on his life by describing himself as "exceedingly vile."[2]

It's difficult to completely blame John for his behavior. Losing his mother (whom he deeply loved) at the age of six and being raised by a distant and extraordinarily strict father who was largely absent due to a demanding travel schedule, the lack of nurture and support in his early years left understandable scars. The loss of his mother also marked the loss of a spiritual and educational influence. John was a bright young boy, but after his mother's death his intellect was largely ignored or misdirected. Lacking continued education, John followed the career path of his father, pursuing the hard life of a seaman. Struggling with bouts of depression, John was inconsistent and unstable. Hired and fired repeatedly, he lacked stability and friendships. Engaging in untold acts of destruction and disgrace, he did not have a life of purpose, much less significant influence. He lacked a sense of direction.

And yet John was uncomfortable with the idea that he wasn't meant for more. He longed for his life to count for something greater. There had to be more purpose and meaning; he just didn't know where to find either one.

After years of aimlessness, John confronted the shaky foundation upon which he had built his identity. He recognized his influence could continue down a road of destruction, or he could change course and discover his God-given influence. John's path led him to a life of significant clout, influence that has probably impacted even you. John Newton's influence lives on through the sacred words that he penned in the hymn "Amazing Grace."

I want my life to matter, and I have always felt that way. Influence is a core longing of our hearts, and I believe it is something God desires for us to pursue. The trouble is that pretty early on we set off on the wrong foot in search of our clout.

Let's play a game for a minute.

Pretend that you and I meet for the first time, and after I ask your name and swap the basics of introductions, my next question is, "Who are you?" How would you respond? The one rule of the game is that you can't tell me what you do. I don't want to know that you're a businessman, a stay-at-home mom, a teacher, a lawyer, or a student. I want to know who you are without hearing what you do or what hat you ordinarily wear. Who are you *really*?

Not so easy, is it?

You see, we've been conditioned to skip over the most basic definition of our influence. We've been taught to define ourselves by what we do rather than who we are. Our clout is entangled in our performance, our experiences, our perceptions of what others expect of us, our talents, our mistakes—the list goes on. It's the most basic identity issue, yet we often don't realize it.

Does this sound familiar?

"Susie, show Aunt Mary how you can count to ten."

"Timmy, recite your ABCs for Grandma."

As soon as Susie and Timmy perform their newly acquired skill, the spectators (aka family) erupt in applause and verbal praise for what they've done—not for who they are.

"Johnny, what do you want to be when you grow up?" When Johnny responds with doctor, firefighter, or policeman, everyone praises him heartily, and Johnny begins his quest to live up to the great expectations of others.

See how early we begin to define who we are by external factors and others' expectations? Herein lies the dilemma. We learn to describe ourselves by our roles and responsibilities rather than by our unique God-given influence. It's not that any of these things are bad. It's part of life. Having accomplishments and goals is important to succeeding in life and even fulfilling all God has called us to. When we first define ourselves by these external forces, however, we never learn to define who we are without them. As a result, we begin to create a false self that forgoes an understanding of who we really are at our core.

In my counselor's office late one Thursday afternoon, she posed the question to me: "Jenni, who are you?" Trying to understand the question behind the question, I turned it back around on her and said, "Isn't that what you're supposed to be helping me figure out?" I knew that I wasn't going to get off that easily as she flipped open her oversized sketchbook (the sacred journal where she keeps all her clients' deepest secrets in picture form) and began to draw a series of circles, one encompassing the other. She described the rings of this haphazardly sketched lopsided bull's-eye based on Thomas Keating's levels of awareness.[3]

> *We learn to describe ourselves by our roles and responsibilities rather than our unique God-given influence.*

The outer ring was my false self—all the things that I try to be, want to be, and pretend to be in order to get others to approve of me. The next ring was my ordinary life—the things that I do and the things that I hang my worth on (my career, my abilities, and my family). The next ring was my spiritual awareness—the things that are my attempts to grow closer to God (church attendance, prayer, devotions, worship, and so on). And the final ring (the bull's-eye) was my true self. When she asked me to define this core, I was at a loss. Week after week in our meetings she asked me if I could define my true self, and repeatedly I came up short. Essentially she was saying, "Jenni, who are you?" and I had no answer.

Understanding who you are is essential for you to be the person whom God has created you to be and to lead confidently from that core. Each of us has a responsibility to manage our clout. But if you can't truly define it, you will flounder for confidence and significance in elements of your false self.

CONFRONTING OUR CRISIS

As I described earlier, I confronted a crisis of purpose in my late twenties that rattled everything I understood about myself and my calling. A disruption in my plans threw my whole world off-kilter. I lost all confidence in who I was and what I thought I was called to do. Frustrated by my discontentment and the uncertainty that it posed, I set off on a course to try to make sense of what my God-given influence should look like. I thought I had a picture of it, but I was beginning to realize that perhaps I started with the wrong map. I built my influence on a self-made platform and missed the significance that my influence was God-given.

It's easy to get distracted by what God is doing through us and miss what's unraveling inside us. Out of my passion to perform, to measure up, to always succeed, to please everyone, and to achieve every dream, my soul was unraveling inside. I ignored the warning signs. I stuffed the evidence behind excuses. I insulated myself from honest conversations and convinced myself it was all in the name of doing what God had called me to do.

That was the season when Galatians 6:4–5 (msg) grabbed my attention: "Make a careful exploration of who you are and the work you have been given, and then sink yourself into that. Don't be impressed with yourself. Don't compare yourself with others. Each of you must take responsibility for doing the creative best you can with your own life." I found so much hope and so much challenge in those verses. Initially I was struck by the two statements sandwiched in the middle of the passage: "Don't be impressed with yourself. Don't compare yourself with others."

As I continued to ponder this passage, those two warning statements took on even greater meaning than the sins of envy and comparison. The statements represented the clout killers that we've been discussing—fear, comparison, jealousy, scarcity, insecurity, pride, and control. Although I began to identify the replacements that lead to the unleashing of our clout, I recognized that there was more work to do. I had question marks about whether I truly understood the first part of this verse: "Make a careful exploration of who you are and the work you have been given."

> *It's easy to get distracted by what God is doing through us and miss what's unraveling inside us.*

Making a careful exploration of who we are is a journey that takes time and hard work. It involves undergoing extreme pressure and sifting through the sands of our history to uncover our uniqueness, strengths, and God-given influence. While the clout killers we discussed in part 1 have provided hints of the ways that our false self impacts our influence, in part 2 we'll dive into the clout cultivators that will challenge us to discover and unleash the things that will give us a healthy foundation from which our God-given influence can thrive.

EXTERNAL PRESSURES
IMPACTING OUR INFLUENCE

My friend Sami is a bit of an intimidating individual—intimidating for seemingly all the right reasons. She is smart, cultured, and accomplished. A child prodigy who skipped three grades and excelled at swimming, tennis, and piano, Sami has always accomplished anything she set her heart on. At first glance you would assume Sami is completely confident and comfortable with who she is and what she's accomplished. But a heart-to-heart conversation revealed the story of a broken little girl responding to myriad external pressures that shaped her identity from an early age:

> From as early as I could remember, I associated love, confidence, and worth with my performance.
>
> I don't even remember the first time I picked up a tennis racket because my father says I was two years old. I can't tell you the first time I swam an entire length of a pool underwater because it's rumored to be when I was just months old.
>
> That's tough press to live up to, even if it was within my own family, thus starting my lifelong pursuit of affirmation and affection.

Sami's parents divorced when she was seven years old, and as children of divorce often do, she assumed responsibility for an unconscious portion of that failure. Determined to prove her worth to both parents, she committed to work even harder to meet their expectations while also being as little of a burden as possible.

She was bored and unchallenged by kindergarten, so her mother and teachers had her tested. The results showed that she was reading at the ninth-grade level and was already writing in cursive and doing multiplication and division problems. With a mild concern for social implications they collectively agreed to put her in third grade. In addition to proving herself at home, she constantly attempted to measure up to her classmates and prove her worth and significance at school:

I quickly learned to become whoever they wanted me to be . . . and that lesson stuck with me into my teen and college years, especially when it came to romantic relationships.

The obvious problem was that I constantly searched for love and approval in all the wrong places; since I didn't truly know who I was, how could I possibly find someone to love me?

The messages for Sami were inconsistent and relentless:

"You won, but you could have played better."

"If you had just worked a little bit harder, you could have gotten the A instead of an A-."

The problem was that my "good" was never "good enough." I became exhausted trying to continually prove myself. The cycle was never-ending: on one hand I would live in the excitement of my accomplishments, but in the next moment it was tempered with the anxiety of having to repeat that same level of performance or living with the reality of getting seriously ill as a result of pushing myself too hard.

OTHERS' EXPECTATIONS

Our parents mean well. They have so many hopes and dreams for us. They dream the things for us that they were never able to do. They want the best for us. They believe in us. But unintentionally (at least most of the time) they heap a burden of pressure on us that weighs us down with expectation and obligation.

Sami's parents didn't mean to give her a false identity. They saw her potential and wanted the best for their daughter. But the pressure was more than Sami could bear, and without an understanding that her worth had nothing to do with what she did, she experienced a life that was an emotional roller-coaster ride of great accomplishments followed by painful emptiness. She could never stay balanced on the tightrope that was her self-worth.

Maybe it wasn't your parents, but it was another influential adult who heaped a mountain of expectations on you. It could have been your football coach, piano teacher, or Sunday school teacher—a person you greatly admired and respected, someone who saw potential in you. Odds are he had no ill intentions, but the pressure he put on you became a standard by which you measured yourself. If you missed a pass, botched a recital, or forgot your memory verse, his disappointment was evident, and your self-worth took a hit. You recovered from those moments by refusing to disappoint him again. And slowly but surely you and he subconsciously measured your worth by how well you met his expectations.

Have you allowed other people's expectations or dreams to shape who you are? How much of what you do in life is based on a compulsion to please the people around you?

SOCIETY'S NORMS

My earliest childhood memories are some of my greatest glimpses of my true self. I did what I did, and I loved what I loved. I don't remember being criticized for being a tomboy or overly praised for treasuring beautiful things. I could as easily get lost in a good book as I could spend hours wandering the trails of our neighborhood, climbing trees, and discovering wildflowers. I'm fortunate that my story doesn't involve a parent or influential adult who told me my quirky blend of interests was wrong. I was neither praised nor criticized for being me.

Before I learned to hear the voice of God, I learned to hear the voice of the masses.

But I was longing for affirmation. I wanted to know whether being me was right, good, and proper. I longed to be sure that I measured up, that I fit in, that I was good enough. Our longing to belong begins well before we realize it's there. So I unknowingly began to pick up subtleties from culture. The unsaid expectations of others spoke very loudly to my intuitive psyche. Before I learned to hear the voice of God, I learned to hear the voice of the masses.

Psychologists apply the social norms theory when they study the impact of our social circles on our behavior and choices. A *Wall Street Journal* writer shared, "Psychologists are studying how social norms, the often-unspoken rules of a group, shape not just our behavior but also our attitudes. Social norms influence even those preferences considered private, such as what music we like or what policies we support."[4] The norms of society speak quite loudly in our lives and impact our behavior in significant ways.

I'm guessing if you are willing to explore it a bit, you'll see some things about yourself that slowly were buried over time as the norms began to speak to you. Maybe you chose sports over music or art rather than science. Perhaps you chose your college or career path because that was the route all your friends were taking. Maybe you took the stable job over an overseas adventure. Whatever the choice, it's likely that you made it with an understanding about whether your social circle would accept it.

One of the greatest dangers to understanding your true self is allowing the pressures of the norms to squeeze out the very things that make you distinct. Your identity is core to your clout, and when you allow society to define it, you've distorted the picture.

Where have you allowed society to speak too loudly in your life? How might it be holding you back from understanding your unique, God-given influence?

MISTAKES

Making mistakes is one of our deepest fears. Most of us naturally assume that a mistake is a clout killer. However, mistakes can be catalysts for further defining our God-given influence. The outcome rests in our choice of one of two paths: we can allow the mistake to perpetuate our false self, or we can use the mistake to help us further define our true self.

The path of the false self allows the mistake to become another layer of guilt, shame, and condemnation that we hide behind. The mistake becomes another way we define ourselves. Instead of being a circumstance in our lives, it becomes another defining moment for our false self and inhibits us from unleashing our clout.

Or we can choose the path of the true self where the mistake becomes a catalyst for understanding something deeper and truer about who we are. An understanding of what led us to make a mistake can reveal important clues about us. We might find that a clout killer was driving our decision. We might see where others' expectations or society's pressure influenced us to make a decision that was contrary to who we really want to be.

Dave Ramsey is a radical example of someone who allowed a mistake to become a catalyst for defining his God-given influence. With more than five million listeners every week on *The Dave Ramsey Show*[5] and three *New York Times* best-selling books on managing money, it's hard to believe that Dave was broke at one point. Dave explains,

> After losing everything, I went on a quest to find out how money really works, how I could get control of it and how I could have confidence in handling it. I read everything I could get my hands on. I interviewed older rich people, people who made money and kept it. That quest led me to a really, really uncomfortable place: my mirror. I came to realize that my money problems, worries and shortages largely began and ended with the person in my mirror.[6]

The mistakes that led to bankruptcy became the fuel for self-discovery. Dave took what was negative about his story and turned it into a thriving organization that helps others avoid the same mistakes he made. He sums it up this way: "I've paid the 'stupid tax' (mistakes with dollar signs on the end) so hopefully some of you won't have to."[7]

What mistake do you have trouble letting go of? How has

that mistake shaped your future? Have you disqualified your-self from some longing or dream because you feel unworthy to attain it now?

EXPERIENCES

Life throws a lot of curveballs at us. We encounter things we could never plan for—good and bad. But much as we do with other forces, we can cling to our experiences to shape our identities.

Don't you get annoyed with the perpetual name-dropper? You know, the person who always knows someone influen-tial and takes every opportunity to showcase her connections. While this individual has found her worth in being connected to someone she highly esteems, she doesn't realize she's actually diminished her worth in your eyes. You don't value her for her experiences or who she knows. You value her for who she is.

Our experiences really aren't the issue. It's what we choose to do with them.

I didn't realize how much my expe-riences had shaped my view of my worth until the day I no longer worked for the record company I idolized. All of a sudden it hit me that I wouldn't be traveling the world with a popular musician. I wouldn't be able to brag about taking trips to Europe or being invited to superstars' homes. My life was going to take a turn for the ordinary that I hadn't calculated.

Right, wrong, good, bad, beautiful, ugly, tragic, or hope-ful, our experiences really aren't the issue. It's what we choose to do with them. Experiences mark us, and that's unavoidable. But hanging our worth on them is avoidable, and we must resist doing that in order to obtain a true understanding of who we are.

What are the greatest experiences of your life so far? Are you stuck in those moments?

GROWING IN OUR IDENTITY

For years I avoided counseling because I was convinced I didn't need it. Counseling was for people who were *really* messed up. I could work through my issues on my own. Giving in to counseling felt like acknowledging I wasn't strong enough to do it on my own.

Author and teacher Ruth Haley Barton put good words to my issue: "Leadership roles, by their very nature, give a lot of fodder to the ego. To remove ourselves, even for a time, from the very arena where we are receiving so much of our identity can be difficult if not impossible for leaders."[8]

By choosing to go to counseling, I was removing myself from the leadership arena and admitting that I needed someone else. I was loosening my death grip on my identity of being a fully in-control, competent leader and allowing myself to be vulnerably human.

In that time with my counselor I was confronted with some of my greatest fears. Things that I didn't want to admit were lurking under the surface. My attempts to avoid them or mask them were doing more damage to my influence. I realized that issues I was unwilling to acknowledge were hindering what God could do through me.

The careful exploration of our God-given influence is not just about identifying the clout killers; it's also about understanding how God has purposefully designed us by giving us gifts, talents, experiences, and opportunities unlike anyone else's.

To really cultivate our influence, we have to be willing to grow, and sometimes growth involves pain and change. A popular definition of *insanity* is "doing the same thing over and over and expecting a different result." The life of a growing leader is constantly changing. Growth = Change.

If you want to lead a life of influence that impacts the world and those you lead, you have to be willing to confront the issues that hold you back. Don't let what could be great become mediocre because you're not doing the self-evaluation necessary to continue to grow.

> *Don't let what could be great become mediocre because you're not doing the self-evaluation necessary to continue to grow.*

I'll warn you that there isn't an easy formula or a simple step-by-step process. The external forces don't go away once you know how to identify them, but as you learn to define how others' expectations, society's norms, your mistakes, and your experiences have shaped you, you can begin to redefine the picture of your true self. The image will become more vivid each and every day. In addition, you'll know what to do to get back on the right path to discovering and unleashing your God-given influence.

DISCOVERY STEPS

- When you were a kid, what did you want to be when you grew up? Is there anything about that early desire that gives you a glimpse of your unique, God-given influence?
- Have you experienced a crisis of purpose—a season when

what you thought you understood about yourself was challenged?

- How have you allowed others' expectations, society's norms, your mistakes, or your experiences to shape who you are?

CHAPTER 9

DEVELOPING YOUR CONFIDENCE

Our authenticity, as well as our power, is unleashed when we live out our true identity and calling in Christ.

—ALAN AND DEBRA HIRSCH[1]

AS WE ARRIVED AMID A SWARM OF ATTENDEES, each eager to find a parking spot and make his or her way to "the happiest place on earth," I became engrossed in the details that made this multimillion-dollar machine operate. From the exuberant parking attendants to the sincerely helpful ticket takers, my critical eye was having difficulty finding anything to critique about this mammoth operation. Disney World was proving to be true to its reputation, and I was intrigued.

There is a lot of conversation about developing a corporate culture and writing mission statements for the workplace, but very rarely do you see those well-intentioned visions lived out on the fringes of the organization. Disney was different. I had heard legends about "the Walt Disney way," but seeing it in action was proof. When an organization remains true to the design and intention of its creator, something magical happens.

To know yourself you have to know your Creator.

The magic that makes Disney special is also true for you and me. In order to fully understand our plan, our purpose, our intention, our influence—our clout—we have to get to know the one who created us. We have to understand his design and plans. In understanding him, we will better understand ourselves.

> *In order to fully understand our plan, our purpose, our intention, our influence—our clout—we have to get to know the one who created us.*

In Ephesians we learn, "It's in Christ that we find out who we are and what we are living for. Long before we first heard of Christ and got our hopes up, he had his eye on us, had designs on us for glorious living, part of the overall purpose he is working out in everything and everyone" (1:11–12 MSG).

I love that. Long before we heard of him, he had his eye on us. That's a glimpse of how well God knows us. He anticipated us before we even existed. His promises throughout Scripture are numerous:

He knows our names (Ps. 91:14).
He knows how many hairs are on our heads (Luke 12:7).
He knew us before we were conceived in the womb
(Ps. 139:13).
He knows when we sit down and when we get up (Ps. 139:2).
He knows our thoughts and our words before we speak them
(Ps. 139:2, 4).
He knows the plans he has for us (Jer. 29:11).

We are made in his image. He has bestowed us with gifts specific to the purpose for which he has designed us. When we take all of that into consideration, it stands to reason that understanding our God-given influence means getting to know the one who created us. The journey to the center of who we are begins with discovering more about the one who designed us.

Confidence is born in this discovery of one's true self. In truly knowing our Creator we better know ourselves. Once we know our Creator and why he made us the way he did with the unique blend of gifts, talents, experiences, and opportunities, we begin to know his voice; we begin to understand his purpose for us. Most important, the journey to the core of who we are teaches us to release what we cling to for a false sense of confidence. We learn to find confidence in who we are because of him. His voice becomes more and more familiar, and we begin to step more confidently into our God-given influence.

I was eight years old when my family started attending church. It didn't take long to see the positive impact this new-found faith in God was having on our lives. As a result I was eager to learn everything I could. I braved the dark, dreary basement rooms of our quaint little church to attend Sunday school each week. The teachers changed from time to time, but the lessons never got old for me. From the typical Old Testament stories of Adam and Eve, Noah, and Moses to the New Testament miracles of Jesus, I soaked in every word.

One story that I don't recall ever hearing back then, however, was the story of Deborah. I stumbled upon her story a few years ago when I was making a concerted effort to learn more about the great women of the Bible. Deborah's story in the book of Judges is short; one chapter is devoted to her influence, and one chapter celebrates how God came through for her and the Israelites. It's no wonder that this story was often missed in our Sunday school studies.

Deborah's story reveals a woman who knew who she was and boldly led from her God-given influence. As I read her story I envied her clout. She displayed confidence in hearing God's voice and confidence in leading the Israelites well.

DEBORAH'S STORY

Deborah was a judge of Israel when King Jabin and the Canaanite army were oppressing the nation. With little means to retaliate, Israel was weak and defenseless. Solving petty disputes among her people was a typical day in Deborah's life as a leader. I imagine it was a gloomy and hopeless existence.

But something changed. Deborah sent for Barak, the leader of the nearly extinct Israelite army and declared to him, "The LORD, the God of Israel, commands you: 'Go, take with you ten thousand men of Naphtali and Zebulun and lead them up to Mount Tabor. I will lead Sisera, the commander of Jabin's army, with his chariots and his troops to the Kishon River and give him into your hands'" (Judg. 4:6–7).

Before we go any further in the story, I have to pause to point out one of the most important things about Deborah's story. She made a very simple but powerful statement: "The LORD, the God of Israel, commands you" (v. 6). When was the last time you told someone on your team, "The LORD, the God of Israel, commands you"? I don't know about you, but I can't remember a time in my life when I felt so confident God had spoken that I would give direction so strongly. When I think God is speaking to me, I don't often say it so boldly. I offer disclaimers: "I *think* God is asking me to do this," or "This *seems* to be God's will for us."

This is an important key to Deborah's influence and leadership. How did she so confidently know that was God's command? It wasn't as if it was a simple command either. History tells us that the Israelites had been under the oppression of the Canaanites for twenty years and that the Canaanites had stripped them of all their weapons. Essentially Deborah was telling ten thousand men to march to their deaths. If I were in her situation, I think I would need a miraculous sign from God to know that he had really given that command, and yet Scripture doesn't tell us that she heard an audible voice or that she was given the command on a written tablet as Moses was. How was she so confident of God's voice?

With a few persuasive pep talks and compelling vision casting, Deborah and Barak somehow convinced ten thousand men to go to battle without weapons. In the heat of the moment Deborah still didn't waver in her confidence in God's promise as she reminded Barak, "Go! This is the day the LORD has given Sisera into your hands. Has not the LORD gone ahead of you?" (v. 14). Imagine how you would feel at this moment. Not only has God given you a daunting command, but you've also somehow recruited everyone to follow you. People's lives were on the line, and yet she didn't falter. She didn't hesitate. She didn't shrink back. She accompanied Barak with their army into battle and ultimately experienced the victory that God had promised.

I want that kind of confidence, don't you?

CULTIVATING CONFIDENCE

Where did Deborah get this courage, this clout? I'm sure this wasn't the fairy tale life every little girl dreams of having. Her career goals probably didn't include leading the Israelites during a time of oppression, and I can't imagine she ever anticipated leading ten thousand men possibly to their deaths.

I have to believe it was rooted and grounded in her relationship with God. We can make assumptions that as a prophetess and judge, she must have displayed an unswerving devotion to God. To know God's voice and to follow it with such assurance could come only from a true understanding of the influence that God had designed her for. It takes each of us back to that journey to the core, to the true self so intricately woven with our Creator that his voice isn't foreign, but so well known we have no reason to doubt it.

> *To know God's voice and to follow it with such assurance could come only from a true understanding of the influence that God had designed her for.*

It's not just Deborah's confidence that is inspiring, but it's the result of that confidence and the impact it had on those she led. Her story concludes with a statement about the impact of her influence: "Then the land had peace forty years" (Judg. 5:31).

God's people experienced peace for forty years because Deborah led from her God-given influence. That is the power of understanding who we are and the work we've been given. The confidence found there not only impacts us but also radically impacts those whom we are called to lead.

Paul challenged us with this perspective: "I count my life

of no value to myself, so that I may finish my course and the ministry I received from the Lord Jesus" (Acts 20:24 HCSB). What would it look like to be that confident in your God-given influence?

I believe with all my heart that God calls each of us to great things. His plans and purposes for us are beyond our wildest imaginations. But they will simply be imaginations and unmet expectations if we skip over this deep understanding of who we are in him. It begins and ends there. We are nothing apart from him.

The best place to start is to think about how you most naturally connect with God. Do you connect with God through nature, worship, reading, or contemplation? Know and understand this about yourself, and then make space for it in your life. My pastor, Pete Wilson, often says, "What matters to our hearts, we build into our lives." Knowing God has to matter to us in such a way that we build it into our lives.

I love to run. A good run provides tremendous stress relief to me while also keeping my heart healthy and my body fit (justification for my multitasking self). But ten years ago if you had told me that I would run more than a mile at a time, I would have said that you were crazy, and I certainly wouldn't have ever believed that I was capable of completing three half marathons. But my competitive nature kicked in a few years ago when my friend Rachel suggested our group of friends train for the Country Music 1/2 Marathon together. She convinced us it would be bonding time, and "we could always walk it if we have to." Well, my pride couldn't handle the idea of resorting to walking, so I attacked that training with crazy intensity. Running became a religious part of my routine, and it has been ever since then. Now I can't imagine not making time for my three weekly runs. I go a little stir-crazy when I miss a run. You could say it matters to my heart, so I've built it into my life.

I wish I could tell you that I've given the same intensity to developing my relationship with God. I've been far more inconsistent in this area. Perhaps it's because my spiritual growth doesn't have the immediate effects I see from logging an extra mile or improving my best time. Or is it possible that I haven't grasped how significant my relationship with God is to discovering and unleashing my God-given influence?

What would it look like if we built time with God into our lives the way I build in time for running? What if I carved out the same amount of time with the same deliberateness and sacredness? You may not be so purposeful about running or exercising, but I guarantee it's something. Understanding the significance of this foundation is essential for leadership clout to thrive.

We Need Time

For our tenth wedding anniversary my husband, Merlyn, and I took a marvelous trip to England and Ireland, just the two of us. While I took in the breathtaking scenery and dreamed of being a princess in one of the many castles we passed, my husband morphed into the Stig from the BBC show *Top Gear*, attempting to clock his best time on the narrow, hilly, and crazy curvy roads of southern Ireland. I said an extra prayer of thanks every time we arrived safely at our destination. Although most of our driving was a complete blur, the Stig frequently had to slow down for the flocks of sheep crossing the road. I kept wondering who was responsible for the fluffy little guys. How did they know where they belonged? Curiosity got the best of me, so I went to my trusted source, Google, to learn more. There are some methods for marking sheep, but the shepherds mostly rely on training the sheep to know their voices (or signals). In essence it's all about the relationship between sheep and shepherd. Sheep are skittish creatures, yet they can be trained to know and respond to their shepherd. It just takes time.

That's the promise of Jesus recorded in John 10:14: "I am the good shepherd; I know my sheep and my sheep know me." It is possible to know God. We gradually get to know our Shepherd by spending time with him. The more time we spend with him, the more comfortable we get with God's voice. It is possible to train ourselves to learn to hear God's voice.

Time is such a scarce commodity in our culture. Not having enough time can become an easily acceptable excuse for not knowing God's voice better. But one thing that seems to be consistent for some of the greatest spiritual leaders in history is that they devoted themselves to spending time with God. In a biography about the life of Hudson Taylor, a British missionary to China, his son and daughter-in-law described the lengths to which Taylor went to make time to read and study God's Word:

> It was not easy for Mr. Taylor, in his changeful life, to make time for prayer and Bible study, but he knew that it was vital. Well do the writers remember traveling with him month after month in northern China, by cart and wheelbarrow, with the poorest of inns at night. Often with only one large room for coolies and travelers alike, they would screen off a corner for their father and another for themselves, with curtains of

some sort; and then, after sleep at last had brought a measure of quiet, they would hear a match struck and see the flicker of candlelight which told that Mr. Taylor, however weary, was poring over the little Bible in two volumes always at hand. From two to four A.M. was the time he usually gave to prayer; the time when he could be most sure of being undisturbed to wait upon God. That flicker of candlelight has meant more to them than all they have read or heard on secret prayer; it meant reality, not preaching but practice.[2]

To understand our God-given influence and to unleash our clout, we must arrange our lives to make time to hear from God. Maybe it's praying while taking a brisk walk or morning run; maybe it's listening to worship music to and from work; maybe it's reading the Bible late at night by candlelight. Whatever you do, however you do it, make time.

KNOWING IS NOT ENOUGH

Knowing God and knowing God's voice aren't enough if they aren't accompanied by obedience.

"You're gonna be in big trouble!" That exclamation was a consistent part of our communication as kids growing up. We knew our mom's voice and her wishes, but that didn't mean we always obeyed them. We were usually trying to find a way around her direction when one us of would pipe up, "You're gonna be in big trouble!" In other words, "I'm gonna tell!"

Likewise, knowing God and knowing God's voice aren't

enough if they aren't accompanied by obedience. That's why Deborah's story is so dynamic. Not only did she know God's voice, but she also obeyed it even when she might not have completely understood it. Even if she was gripped by fear, she obeyed. Even when they didn't have the weapons they needed to protect themselves, she obeyed. Even if she felt inadequate and insecure, she obeyed. Even if pride started to give her a false sense of confidence, she obeyed. Even if she was tempted to compare this battle to other battles faced by God's people (some leading to defeat), she obeyed. Even if she was tempted to control the situation, she obeyed. Deborah confronted her clout killers and remained obedient to God's voice and call for her life.

Where do you struggle the most: knowing or obeying? Do you believe God's promises about how well he knows you? Do you believe that he wants to know you? Do you want to know him better? Are you beginning to recognize the relationship between knowing God and understanding your God-given influence? What small step could you take this week to spend time with God in an effort to better know him?

Knowing God brings clarity to your clout.

Knowing God brings clarity to your clout. Much like the boldness and confidence Deborah displayed, our God-given influence is unleashed when we confidently know God's voice and are obedient to follow it.

Where are you struggling with obedience? Has God called you to something, but you are reluctant to do it? What do you need to do to take a step toward obedience? What is God asking of you, and how can you say yes to him?

What do you think is distracting you from being confident

in your God-given influence? Is it knowing his voice? Is it being obedient to his voice? Is it needing a better understanding of how he has wired and gifted you? Are you being held back by fear, comparison, jealousy, scarcity, insecurity, pride, or control?

It is possible to know God's voice, and it is possible to obey and lead from a place of security and confidence of who you are in him. Your true self is God's presence in you. The core of who you are—your true self—is his.

DISCOVERY STEPS

- Go back and reread God's promises about you from page 128. What other promises from Scripture remind you of God's desire to have a relationship with you?
- Schedule a consistent time in your calendar to talk to God each week. Make sure it's in keeping with how you best connect with God, and guard this time.
- Share with a trusted friend, pastor, or counselor the area in which you are having trouble being obedient. Ask this person to pray with you and hold you accountable to it.
- Stop making excuses, and try to identify solutions or small incremental steps that you can take toward being obedient.

CHAPTER 10

DEFINING YOUR MISSION

I think in some of us there is an urge to do certain things, and if we did not do them, we would feel that we were not fulfilling the job which we had been given opportunities and talents to do.

—ELEANOR ROOSEVELT[1]

CROSS POINT, THE CHURCH I SERVE IN NASHVILLE, Tennessee, has an amazing ministry to underresourced people, especially the homeless population. Our dynamic team of volunteers is gifted at walking through life with troubled individuals. I am always amazed by the stories behind the faces they serve. One particular story got my attention.

Mike didn't fit the stereotype of many homeless people we meet. Mike wasn't using drugs. He wasn't drinking. He was living an uncommitted life. Mike was exceptionally smart. He had a doctorate degree, had been a professor at a prestigious college, and at one time was living the American Dream with two kids, a beautiful wife, a big home in the suburbs, and the social scene to support it all. Most of us would have envied the life that Mike was leading.

But in the rat race to do it all and be it all, Mike lost himself and his family, and ultimately he lost hope. The pressure to perform—to do—gradually eroded his relationships with his wife and daughters. In all his doing, he lost purpose. His work was a reaction to a need—the perpetual need for more. That inexhaustible need ultimately starved his relationships and ruined Mike's life.

In all his doing, Mike lost the ability to be. Now Mike just sits under the bridge, occasionally chats with his homeless friends, and wanders the streets for a few bucks. Mike has no motivation to do anything because he has no hope and no purpose. It all seems meaningless to him.

Mike has all the ability in the world. He has done notable things, but I'm guessing that Mike no longer knows who he is nor does he believe that he has a worthwhile purpose to fulfill.

A crisis of purpose robs us of hope when who we are and the work we've been given become splintered.

When we *do* without an understanding of who we are or why we do what we do, a separation occurs. Our purpose becomes separated from our actions. Rather than work in alignment with our God-given influence, we work against it. A crisis of purpose robs us of hope when who we are and the work we've been given become splintered. At one point, Mike had a lot of clout, but lack of purpose for what he was doing diminished his hope. Like Mike, we give up when we lose hope.

We must discover our core identity to unleash our true, God-given influence. Forces are working against us to derail our purpose and diminish our hope. If we haven't done the exploring, we leave ourselves vulnerable to despair and hopelessness.

Joel Manby described his crisis of purpose in his book *Love Works*. An extraordinarily successful businessman, Joel was on the brink of burnout, continuous travel was straining his family relationships, and he was miserably discontented with the work he was doing:

> Life hadn't turned out as I had hoped. I had worked hard, getting straight As in college while playing varsity football and baseball, graduating from Harvard Business School, and then climbing the ladder at GM, which had culminated in a rise to the top spot at Saab North America at thirty-six years old.
>
> Yet as I sat in that one-room apartment in California, I was at rock bottom according to the metrics that truly mattered to me. How could I be excited about a work lifestyle that would destroy my family? I didn't know what to do next.[2]

Joel's story seems all too familiar, doesn't it? It sounds a lot like the story of Mike, the homeless guy. The difference in their stories is what they chose to do at the moment when they faced their crisis of purpose. Mike chose to give up; Joel chose to dig in. Joel understood that his work had to be redefined by who he was and who God had designed him to be. He recognized that his God-given influence was defined not by what he was doing but by who he was being. Joel recognized that who he was and the work he was doing had to be inextricably linked.

He explained it this way: "*Be* goals are about defining the kind of people we want to be instead of what we want to accomplish. The great thing about *be* goals is that they are within our control. And, even more importantly, when we live in a manner that is consistent with those goals, we discover contentment and peace such as we have never known before—contentment and peace that we experience independent of the day-to-day numerical imperatives of work."[3]

As leaders, we are naturally driven to *do*. This is how our clout most commonly gets hijacked. Because we are compelled by doing, we miss out on the exploration of being. We separate these two things and find ourselves disconnected from the core of our influence.

The daunting question then is, So what about what we do?

It is and it isn't about what we do. Our God-given influence isn't all about what we do, and yet we do have a purpose to accomplish. We don't *do* to earn God's love or acceptance or approval, but we *do* as a response to the love and grace God has freely given us. We *do* out of love rather than out of obligation. Our doing is a response of thankfulness to God's doing in our lives.

REDEFINING WORK

The account of creation in Genesis 1 gives us a first glimpse of our God-given influence. We see God's original plan for the work that he gave Adam and Eve to do: "God blessed them and said to them, 'Be fruitful and increase in number, fill the earth and subdue it. Rule over the fish of the sea and the birds of the air and over every living creature that moves on the ground' " (v. 28).

I've often mistaken work as a consequence of our sin. The serpent, the fruit, the question, the consequence. After the tragedy in the garden, the ground was cursed, and work entered the world. But when you look more closely at the first chapter of Genesis we're told that God gave us work to do: have babies, subdue the earth, and rule over the fish, the birds, and every living creature. Before the fall. Before sin messed things up, work was still a part of our lives. God attributed significance to work even before it was a result of our sin. We were made to work.

The work we were given from the beginning of our existence was to "fill the earth and subdue it." Think about the significance of this. God spent six days creating this unbelievable creation, and he immediately handed its stewardship over to us.

When I was a kid I loved Legos. I'm not talking about mild interest. I mean obsession! Most Christmases and birthdays I got a new Lego kit. Dad devoted a corner of the basement to my city of Legos that multiplied with each new project. I meticulously put together the hospital or the new fire station precisely according to the detailed instructions. The completion of my new creation was a momentous occasion for me. I took extraordinary pride in my Lego city, but I never turned the keys over to someone else. I allowed others to participate in enjoying it with me, but I never granted them the privilege of being responsible for it.

The work we've been given to do is not about toil and labor but about responsibly unleashing the influence he's given us.

Imagine the care and intentionality that God must have devoted to his creation. Then imagine how significant it was for him to entrust it all into our care. The work we've been given is an extraordinary gift that God has entrusted to us.

Our modern view equates work with punishment. It's a necessary evil—we work to survive. It's the place we go more than forty hours a week to pay the bills and provide for our indulgences. Work is rarely considered a privilege. It's a means to an end—safety, security, provision, and rewards.

This is where some redefinition is required. The work God has given us isn't an employer-employee transaction. It's not a job. It's not punching a time clock or meeting performance expectations. It's a relationship where the one who deeply knows us and loves us entrusts us with his prized possessions to equip us to partner with him for eternal significance. Our work is far more than our jobs; our work is our influence in action. Our work is the collection of everything we do. It's the tangible actions of who we are. It's how we lead, it's how we parent, it's how we manage our homes, it's how we caretake our relationships, it's how we exercise, it's how we have fun, and it's how we go about our day from the time we wake to the time we lie down to sleep. The "work we've been given" is the actions that make up our day.

Paul wrote, "We are God's handiwork, created in Christ Jesus to do good works, which God prepared in advance for us to do" (Eph. 2:10). Two very significant things are going on in this verse. First, we are God's handiwork. He took great care in creating us and forming us. King David responded to God's creation and provision with these words:

> *I praise you because I am fearfully and wonderfully made;*

your works are wonderful,
I know that full well.

(Ps. 139:14)

Second, we are created to do good works, which God prepared for us in advance. He has a plan to use our influence to do wonderful things. He has already created the instruction manual.

GATHERING OUR PIECES

By the time I reached middle school, my obsession with Lego city had diminished greatly (it would have been a little awkward if it hadn't). I came home one Sunday afternoon following a slumber party weekend with friends and discovered that my little sister had taken a special interest in my abandoned Legos. Neatly organized and well-constructed city streets had become a pile of completely unrecognizable plastic rubble. Her creative curiosity took her down a path of destruction that was irreparable. Without the original instructions, Lego city lost all its value and purpose.

Life may seem like a pile of rubble to you. You have all the pieces, but you don't know how to make them work together. Maybe you started constructing a seemingly perfect life, only to have someone or some circumstance tear it apart. Some have forced the pieces together into an awkward mess. Others have never had a vision for what your life and your work could be.

I define *God-given influence* as "the collection of nuances that make you unique." God has given each one of us a specific set of gifts, talents, personality, and experiences. This one-of-a-kind collection is your clout, and it's been given to you for the specific work God has for you to do. To discover and unleash your God-given influence, you have to hunt for all the pieces.

SPIRITUAL GIFTS

I love gifts, both getting and giving them. I obsess about finding the perfect gift for others, and I enjoy seeing a friend's eyes light up when she opens a gift that she truly wanted. If you're familiar with Gary Chapman's book *The 5 Love Languages*, you understand that gifts is one of my love languages.[4] It's how I best give and receive love.

I think I was in high school when I learned that God gives special gifts to those who have chosen to follow him. Realizing that was like discovering another beautifully wrapped gift hidden under the Christmas tree waiting for me to open it!

Numerous places throughout the New Testament identify spiritual gifts. First Corinthians 12 notes the gifts of wisdom, knowledge, faith, healing, prophecy, discernment, apostleship, teaching, helps, and administration. Romans 12 adds these to the list: serving, encouragement, giving, and leadership.

Understanding the spiritual gifts God has given you is an important step in defining your clout. Have you ever done a spiritual gifts assessment? If not, many resources can help you discover your gifts. I've listed an option in the resource section in the back of this book. If you do know your gifts, how are you developing them? First Timothy 4:14 instructs, "Do not neglect your gift." Spiritual gifts are gifts of grace from God to us. It's as if he's giving us a head start on the character traits and qualities that he desires for us to live out.

Spiritual gifts are gifts of grace from God to us.

The apostle Paul wrote that we've been given these gifts to serve the body of Christ (Eph. 4). Each of us contributes individual and different gifts in order to help all believers grow in unity, faith, knowledge, and maturity. Consider an effective team. When the leader casts a vision well, the administrators handle the money properly, the support staff serves conscientiously, and individual team members use their knowledge to do their jobs efficiently, you see a team that thrives. If someone attempts to do something for which he or she is unqualified, the whole team suffers.

When we use our gifts to benefit others, we help to accomplish God's plan and purpose. This is how we begin to live out the work we've been given. Our part of this equation is essential to God's bigger picture. Our influence grows as we know and understand our contribution.

TALENTS

Talents are often classified as special aptitude in athletics, creativity, or artistic abilities. You might have a knack for cooking. Maybe you could throw a perfect pass before you could walk. You could be the one person in your family who can actually carry a tune. Maybe you have an uncanny ability to solve problems.

Talents come in all shapes and sizes. They are the idiosyncrasies that give you an edge. They differ from spiritual gifts in that you are born with talents, whereas spiritual gifts are given to believers to help accomplish the mission of the gospel. Talents are abilities that are God-given to make you unique. We all have them. Yours may be undeveloped, but once you tap into it, you find that you have an unusual ability to do something better than the next person.

Talents are best identified by reflecting on these and similar questions:

What was your favorite game or activity as a child?
What do others commonly praise you for?
What were your favorite subjects in school?
What extracurricular activities do you enjoy?
What would you choose to do if you had a day all to
    yourself with no commitments or obligations?

Talents may be things that you easily dismiss about yourself. You don't identify them as talents because they aren't difficult for you. Sure, you might have done some work to refine them if you've chosen to fully develop those talents. But operating from your talents feels natural and comfortable.

Well-known author Marcus Buckingham refers to developing your talents as identifying your strengths.[5] Buckingham's strengths movement uses the Clifton StrengthsFinder tool to help people identify their top five strengths and then equips them to understand how to live and operate more fully from them. His perspective is that we're the most fully alive and engaged when we make a concerted effort to play to our strengths in every area of life. (If you're interested in taking the StrengthsFinder assessment, more information is included in the resource section at the back of this book.)

Your talents are another piece in the picture of your influence. They define more ways that you can accomplish the work you've been given. Your talents position you for influence in areas where others may not have the same opportunity.

PERSONALITY

How would others describe your personality? Quirky, witty, serious, fun, shy, outgoing? The adjectives to describe this part of someone's uniqueness are endless.

I was excited about becoming an aunt, but I was surprised at how quickly this little niece of mine captured my heart. My favorite thing about watching her grow is seeing her personality come alive. I see bits of her mom and her dad, I see our family's stubborn streak rear its ugly head, and I see traits that are uniquely hers.

Personality traits are the crazy things about us that make people exclaim, "That is so you!" One of my favorite photos from my wedding day is a candid black-and-white shot that someone caught of me just minutes before I was to walk down the aisle. Fully decked out in my dress and veil, I was sitting on a small chair in the Sunday school classroom of the church and writing checks to all the vendors hired for the day. Everyone who sees that picture says, "That is so Jenni. All business all the time." During one of the biggest moments of my life, I was still taking care of business. Thorough attention to detail and the ability to juggle many things at once are distinct parts of my personality.

The problem with personality is that it's so core to who you are, you may not recognize the unique parts of it. It's easy to miss how some idiosyncratic tendencies can be useful in assembling the puzzle of who you are and the natural clout you have. A quick way to identify the key characteristics of your personality is to do an informal poll of your friends and family. Ask them to give you the first word that comes to their minds to describe your personality, write down those words, and pay attention to what is repeated.

Your personality brings color to your work. Where spiritual gifts and talents create the outline and structure, personality brings the picture of you to life.

The Purpose of Our Work

Even with a better understanding of what work is, some days I still ask *why*. Many days it still feels overwhelming. I get lost in all the *doing* and have difficulty understanding the purpose. I start plotting strategies for alleviating the stressors. For a moment I wonder whether all the work is worth it.

That moment of doubt is a critical point. It's the decision point where you choose the path that Mike, the homeless man, chose, or you choose a path of hope and purpose as Joel did. But let's be honest. Choosing Mike's path seems a lot easier some days, especially if you don't understand the purpose you're working toward.

Let's consider reasons for the purpose of our work:

To Glorify God

Jesus said, "Let your light shine before others, that they may see your good deeds and glorify your Father in heaven" (Matt. 5:16). When we do good, God gets the glory. In one story Jesus told us about a blind man who others believed was blind because he sinned, but Jesus clarified: "This happened so that the works of God might be displayed in him" (John 9:3). Our lives are arenas for God's work to be displayed. As we take the pieces of the puzzles of our lives and put them together, we create opportunities for his work to be displayed in us.

To Benefit Others

Taking our gifts, talents, and personalities to the world benefits others. Consider the loss if great leaders didn't step up to lead, talented musicians didn't create inspired music, administrators didn't organize, or the strong didn't protect and defend us. Paul urged us, "I want you to stress these things, so that those

We starve the world when we withhold our influence.

who have trusted in God may be careful to devote themselves to doing what is good. These things are excellent and profitable for everyone" (Titus 3:8). Think of the people closest to you. What would be missing in your life if they didn't share their distinct gifts, talents, and personalities? What would they be missing if you weren't a part of their world? We starve the world when we withhold our influence.

To Make God Smile

My friends have some of the most amazing kids. I love attending their ballet recitals, gymnastic competitions, and football and soccer games. I love to be there to cheer them on. Seeing them give their best makes me beam with pride.

Sometimes it's difficult for me to imagine that God shares these emotions. I'm not sure why. It's just hard to wrap my mind around the idea of a deity who fully understands us. But given the fact that he created every emotion we feel, I suspect he has a pretty good understanding. I've come to believe that when we make a careful exploration and are fully thriving in the work we've been given, we make God smile because "it is God who is at work in [us], both to will and to work for His good pleasure" (Phil. 2:13 NASB). He finds pleasure when we're operating within his will and the work he's given us. That word *pleasure* refers to "a source of delight or joy."[6] God is in the audience of life beaming with delight and joy as we go about our work.

To Give Us Hope

Our work is discovering and unleashing our God-given influence. It's infusing our personalities with the implementation of our talents and gifts. It's living out our clout. Philippians 1:6 (NASB) assures us, "He who began a good work in you will perfect it until the day of Christ Jesus." I love the part "perfect it until . . ." It conveys an ongoing process. The perfecting continues. Those talents, gifts, and crazy parts of our personalities continue to be refined. There is hope in that. There is purpose in that.

Remember how Mike lost hope? Mike lost hope because he either forgot or never understood the purpose behind his work. But "we are God's handiwork, created in Christ Jesus to do good works, which God prepared in advance for us to do" (Eph. 2:10). Our work matters. It is significant. It has purpose.

Now it's time to sink ourselves into it!

DISCOVERY STEPS

- Do you confuse work with your employment?
- Can you define your spiritual gifts and talents? If not, take time to discover what they are.
- How do you and others describe your personality?
- Which purpose of work is the most difficult for you to believe: to glorify God, to benefit others, to make God smile, or to give us hope?

CHAPTER 11

DETERMINING YOUR PASSION

*I tell you that as long as I can conceive something better
than myself I cannot be easy unless I am striving to bring
it into existence or clearing the way for it.*

—George Bernard Shaw[1]

FOR THE TWO YEARS THAT MATT HASSELBECK was the quarterback for the Tennessee Titans I had the privilege of observing an inspiring leader in action. One would think it would be enough that he was graced with a tremendous amount of influence from his impressive career and his strong pedigree. But Matt understands that his clout is so much more than the title he carries or the winning passes he's thrown. Matt's God-given influence goes beyond the jersey he wears. He understands that the work he has been given is not about winning performances but about using his influence for good. At the core of who Matt is, is a passion for sharing the hope of Christ with others. Whether it's supporting a nonprofit fund-raiser, having a one-on-one conversation with a teammate, or inviting someone to attend church with him, Matt is always looking for ways to make his clout count.

In Luke 12 Jesus shared a series of parables about the importance of stewardship. There is the parable of the rich fool who accumulated a mass of wealth and then told himself, "Take life easy; eat, drink and be merry" (Luke 12:19). Gifted with the ability to multiply what God had given him, he squandered it by consuming it all himself. God called him a fool for his selfishness.

In another parable, Jesus highlighted the importance of the servants' keeping their lamps burning and being ready for whenever their master returned (Luke 12:35–40). Throughout the sermon Jesus was preaching, he told intense stories in which he challenged us about the importance of being prepared and ready. He chided the rich fool for storing up treasure for himself and not being generous. He warned the servants about keeping the master's estate prepared for his return. He spoke often about our responsibility to do the best with what we're given.

What is most fascinating to me is that within this passage where Jesus challenged us to be ready, to be prepared, and to be responsible, he also warned against worry or fear. In the middle of challenging us to be good stewards he reminded us of how he takes care of us:

> I tell you, do not worry about your life, what you will eat; or about your body, what you will wear. For life is more than food, and the body more than clothes. Consider the ravens: They do not sow or reap, they have no storeroom or barn; yet God feeds them. And how much more valuable you are than

birds! Who of you by worrying can add a single hour to your life? Since you cannot do this very little thing, why do you worry about the rest? (Luke 12:22–26)

An interesting dance takes place in this chapter. God challenges us to own our part while reminding us he is in control. I interpret this as a responsibility that he has placed into our hands—a partnership. He is inviting us into his work but protecting us from feeling the weight of the world on our shoulders.

The words of Luke 12:48 have challenged my leadership for years: "From everyone who has been given much, much will be demanded; and from the one who has been entrusted with much, much more will be asked."

God has given us much. From the purposeful way that he created us with unique experiences, to our gifts, talents, and personalities, not to mention that the majority of readers of this book and I have the resources to supply a roof over our heads and sufficient food and clothes, we have been extraordinarily blessed.

So if we've been given much, what exactly is required? What does it look like to take responsibility for all God has blessed us with? What does it mean to be prepared? How are we to avoid the pitfall of the foolish rich man and be ready and prepared as faithful servants?

EXCHANGING OWNERSHIP
FOR STEWARDSHIP

There is something special about the feeling of ownership. I vividly remember pulling away from the car lot the day I bought my first car—a 1992 maroon Saturn SL1. I saved diligently for that car, and I felt pride in knowing that it was all mine. I didn't even care that it lacked air-conditioning, although I was headed to the triple-digit temperatures of Nashville, Tennessee, in the dead of summer! It was mine. That was all that mattered.

The same exhilarating feeling happened when my husband and I purchased our first home. There was no end to the home improvement projects we had in mind to make the place our own.

Ownership provides privilege, pride, freedom, and a sense of responsibility. But ownership also has a dark side. It feeds the illusion of control. The idea that it's ours may cause us to drift toward an attitude of entitlement. The more invested I am in something, the more costly it will be to lose. The more control I have acquired, the more insecure I become about things not going my way.

Stewardship, on the other hand, recognizes that I've been entrusted with something valuable and I have a responsibility to give it my best care. I don't own it, but I've been given an amazing privilege.

Set this book down for a minute, and hold your hands side by side, palms up as if you are cradling something valuable. In these hands God has placed your gifts, talents, experiences, and opportunities. As a steward, you will keep your hands open and gently hold these items, being sensitive to how God leads and directs you. You will carry them confidently yet gently.

But what happens when we become complacent, bored, frustrated, or disinterested? When we face these challenges, we can easily get tired of holding up our hands. We lose sight of the purpose, and we don't have the energy to keep gently holding them. Before we know it, we've thrown up our hands and walked away.

What about when we become nervous, insecure, threatened, or scared? In these moments our tendency is to tighten our grip. Our fingers curl around it, and we develop such a death grip that we squeeze the life out of it. We become frantic owners grasping for a sense of control.

We have to constantly monitor an attitude of stewardship in our lives. Time and time again I find myself clutching too tightly the gifts, talents, experiences, and opportunities that God has given me to manage. The best way I've learned to combat this tendency in myself is to physically hold my hands up in an open palms posture and pray specifically about the issues that I am desperate to control. We

> *We start squeezing the life out of our God-given influence when we attempt to take over and control.*

start squeezing the life out of our God-given influence when we attempt to take over and control. It's only through an attitude of stewardship that we learn to hold loosely while still assuming our responsibility.

Go with What You Know

Most biblical scholars estimate that David was a teenager when he took on the giant Goliath. While his older brothers were off to battle, serving King Saul against the Philistines, young David was entrusted with taking care of the sheep back home. Occasionally his father sent him to the battle lines to take provisions to his brothers. On one of the supply runs David learned about Goliath's intimidation tactics:

Goliath stood and shouted to the ranks of Israel, "Why do you come out and line up for battle? Am I not a Philistine, and are you not the servants of Saul? Choose a man and have him come down to me. If he is able to fight and kill me, we will become your subjects; but if I overcome him and kill him, you will become our subjects and serve us." Then the Philistine said, "This day I defy the armies of Israel! Give me a man and let us fight each other." On hearing the Philistine's words, Saul and all the Israelites were dismayed and terrified. (1 Sam. 17:8–11)

You know what happened next. David told Saul that he wanted to take on Goliath. Saul's response was probably similar to what I would have said to him: "You are not able to go out against this Philistine and fight him; you are only a young man" (v. 33). David responded with why he was qualified to do what he said. He didn't make excuses for not having military experience or try to convince Saul he was something that he was not. He drew on his life experience to that point as a shepherd. He knew that the experiences God had given him had equipped him in a unique way to take on the giant. Just as he had fended off and killed lions and bears that attacked his sheep, he believed he could kill Goliath. David understood with confidence that God had given him what he needed for this moment.

Then Saul dressed David in his own tunic. He put a coat of armor on him and a bronze helmet on his head. David fastened on his sword over the tunic and tried walking around, because he was not used to them.

"I cannot go in these," he said to Saul, "because I am not

used to them." So he took them off. Then he took his staff in his hand, chose five smooth stones from the stream, put them in the pouch of his shepherd's bag and, with his sling in his hand, approached the Philistine. (vv. 38–40)

This part of the story might be my favorite. Saul did what any good leader would do to prepare David for the battle. Saul relied on what he knew. He equipped David in the same way he would equip himself. If I was David, I would be tempted to take the advice of this older, wiser leader. Even though it felt uncomfortable I would likely heed an expert's opinion. But David followed his own instincts.

I marvel at David's confidence to go with what he knew. He chose to do it his way, trusting in the experiences that specifically equipped him for that moment. He was not trying to be someone else. He was trusting in who he was and the work he had been given.

How many times do you and I face new challenges, and rather than seek clarity on how God has uniquely equipped us, we are tempted to mimic another leader who has gone before us? I don't know about you, but generally my first reaction is to find out how someone else did it and then model my plan accordingly. For much of my life I've assumed that is the right way to approach things. It's not that this approach is wrong, but moving forward without discerning how God has specifically prepared you is like cutting yourself off at the knees. You lose access to a great deal of the power you've been given. Part of how God has equipped you might indeed be with the wisdom of others who have gone before you, and then other times he might have an altogether different route for you in mind, as he did for David.

Notice how David handled the situation. He didn't reject Saul's gear until after Saul suited him up and he had a chance

Sometimes unleashing our God-given influence means confidently doing it our way.

to walk around in it and feel it out. He humbly evaluated how an experienced leader would handle the situation and then compared that against the tools with which he was familiar. With all the information in front of him he made a discerning choice about how he was best equipped to handle the challenge.

Sometimes unleashing our God-given influence means confidently doing it our way. Be humble enough to heed the wisdom of others and evaluate all the options, but be confident in the unique ways that God has equipped you.

START WHERE YOU ARE

For more than a year my office was continuously covered with architectural plans. We were relocating our broadcast campus, and I was leading our efforts to renovate a new building we purchased. To say that I was in over my head would be an understatement, but I quickly learned that everything we did revolved around the plans for the building. We needed the plans to determine budget, to employ a contractor, to meet Metro codes approval, to guide construction, and to clarify every detail related to our new space. We couldn't so much as pick up a hammer without consulting the plans. Without the plans we'd probably still be looking at that building and talking about what it could be but never taking action.

Planning is a critical part of the exploration process. Once you've gathered your tools—gifts, talents, personality, and experiences—how do you organize them into an action plan that allows you to operate from your God-given influence? For many of you, the exploration so far might have caused more frustration. The things that God has given you are extraordinarily exciting and you catch quick glimpses of what your discovery could mean, but reality gets in the way of dreaming about how to put your God-given influence to work.

As we sat down with the architects to create our plan for the new building, I had no idea where to start. Fortunately because they do that for a living, they did. Your plan has to start with where you are. What are the facts of your story? For Cross Point, we clarified our most important ministries, we tallied data on attendance, and we defined the core elements of who we are as a church.

This is the best way for you to approach your plan too. Where are you now? If you haven't already done so, make a list of the gifts, talents, experiences, and opportunities that have contributed to who you are today. Here's an example of my list:

- firstborn
- tomboy
- lover of music and entertainment
- meticulous organizer
- child of divorced parents
- big sister
- piano player
- hard worker
- gift giver

- avid reader
- closet writer
- quiet
- shy child
- ladder climber

Make that list as long as you want. Write out everything that describes you and every experience you believe has shaped you. Do you see any connection or consistencies weaving throughout? Spend time reviewing this list, and ask God to reveal to you anything about this combination that you are not aware of.

Define Where You Want to Go

Now it's time to dream a bit. You have to understand where you are before you can dream about where you're going. Once the architects helped us define our starting point, we had the framework to shape the vision for the future.

What are some of your secret goals or wishes? Those things that seem so audacious that you couldn't possibly share them with someone for fear of being shot down. Do you know what one of mine was? Writing a book. Ever since I was a little girl I've dreamed of writing a book. I started my first manuscript when I was in the third grade. I don't even remember what the story was about, but I vividly remember how sacred it was to me. I secretly carried the dream of writing for

You have to understand where you are before you can dream about where you're going.

many years but was terrified that if I verbalized that dream, others wouldn't affirm it.

Where do you want to go? What do you want to do? Is there a talent you've left dormant that you want to pick up again? What parts of your personality would you love to grow and develop? What influence do you long for? What do you hope to accomplish with your clout?

Plotting where you want to go is much more about changing the course of how you allow your heart and mind to dream. Make a list of things you would love to be true about you. Don't get stuck by the limitations of resources or responsibilities, but filter them through the recognition of the tools that God has given you. For example, if you can't carry a tune, give up the dream of being a Grammy-winning artist. Choose a realistic yet optimistic approach as you build this list. Here are a few items on my list:

- Have a piano at home so I can play for myself and my family.
- Develop greater patience and more compassion for others.
- Learn to balance my drivenness with the ability to have fun.
- Laugh more.

The act of putting ideas to paper moves them from pipe dreams to possibilities. Even in our planning we have to remember to live with open hands. Our plans are really the intention to steward the plans God wants to accomplish through us: "We can make our plans, / but the Lord determines our steps" (Prov. 16:9 NLT).

Although charting the specific steps for the rest of our lives is a daunting and unrealistic goal, I believe there are some ways that we can create the architecture from which we can build our influence.

Personal Vision Statement

I'm a big believer in the importance of having a personal vision statement. Most of us are familiar with vision statements— sometimes called mission statements or purpose statements. The organization that employs you likely has one. The church you attend has one. Most businesses you frequent have one, or they probably wouldn't be in business long. A vision statement defines who you are and why you do what you do.

If McDonald's didn't have a vision to provide "the world's best quick service restaurant experience," the company might on a whim decide to turn into a fancy sit-down restaurant or change course completely and start selling computers. Or if Nike decided to abandon its vision "to bring inspiration and innovation to every athlete in the world" and become a music store, the company would quickly flounder from a divided purpose.

Vision statements give us an anchor for those days we feel that we're floundering.

Vision statements give us an anchor for those days we feel that we're floundering. They put on paper what God has been revealing to us about our influence, and they remind us on the days when we're tempted to compare and compete with others that our purpose is specific and unique to who we are. To try to imitate someone else or chase the latest whim would be contrary to our clout.

Ten years ago my husband was going through his own crisis of purpose. He was reared in a musical family, and everyone expected that he would pursue a career in music. In response to those expectations, he chose that path, and he was exceptional at it. Yet he couldn't shake the nagging feeling that there was more of his clout to explore. His restlessness finally led him to a journey of exploration where he laid aside every expectation and began to dream about what other things he was called and equipped to do. That season led him to discover his deep God-given passion for pursuing justice on behalf of those who can't do it for themselves. His exploration resulted in a complete change of course, and he began his career in law enforcement. Now he uses his musical gifts and talents to serve the church and his passion for justice to serve the community. His crisis of purpose led him to identify additional talents and gifts that may have been left undiscovered.

Your personal vision statement needs to define at the core what God has called you to. It won't be specific to a job or a season. It will be an overarching reflection of who you are. Stephen Covey defined it this way: "A mission statement is your philosophy on how you want to live and captures what contributions you want to make during your lifetime."[2]

Studies show that you are more likely to achieve a goal when you write it down. By writing it down, you are giving yourself something to reflect on during uncertain moments.

Here is my personal vision statement: "To lead, motivate, and mentor others who are pursuing their passion and purpose in life. To encourage, equip, and train people of influence to lead a balanced life in active pursuit of their purpose."

I wrote this statement eight years ago, long before I dreamed I would be leading in the specific way that I am or that I would be writing a book on the subject. Yet that statement is as true today as it was eight years ago when I led my first small group.

If you already have a personal vision statement, take time to reflect on it. If you ordinarily keep it tucked away, put it in a more prominent place so you're reminded of it every day. Based upon what you've discovered about yourself as you've read this book, are there any parts of it you should clarify?

If you've never written a personal vision statement, I encourage you to draft one. Here are suggestions to get you started:

1. Observe the formula. Vision statements are a combination of defining what you do and who is involved. What + Who. My vision statement is two *what* + *who* statements.

What	Who
To lead, motivate, and mentor	others who are pursuing their passion and purpose in life.
To encourage, equip, and train	people of influence to lead a balanced life in active pursuit of their purpose.

2. Brainstorm a list of action words that describe what you feel called to do. Look back through your gifts, talents, and experiences for consistencies and themes. Write them down, and keep refining the list. You may choose to do this over the course of a week as you let yourself live with the words and concepts.

3. Consider who you feel called to serve. From what groups of people do you get energy when you are pouring yourself out

to serve them? Do you love teaching Sunday school? Do you thrive when you're leading a small group? Do you enjoy serving homeless or underresourced people? Do you thrive when you're connecting business leaders? If you're not immediately certain of who you most feel called to serve, take a couple of weeks, and observe your level of engagement in different environments. Your *who* will likely emerge as you watch for it.

4. Start crafting your *whats* and *whos* into statements. Don't be afraid to write several statements until you think you have the right combination. You probably won't get it exactly right the first time you sit down to do it. Take a week, and spend thirty minutes every day refining it until it feels right.

5. Give your statement to a couple of close friends, and ask for their feedback on how well it describes who God has designed you to be. Consider their feedback and how it might apply.

6. Pray over your vision statement. Ask God to affirm or clarify what you've drafted.

7. Place your vision statement somewhere you can read it every day.

Guiding Principles

Now that you have your personal vision statement, you might want to take it a step further. You likely left a lot of great desires and attributes on the cutting-room floor when you narrowed down your vision statement. Creating a list of guiding principles allows you to define the characteristics and qualities that you want to strive to embrace as you live out your vision statement.

Here are my guiding principles:

>I represent a balanced lifestyle.
>I value the relationships with my family and friends and diligently seek to grow these relationships.
>I pursue excellence in all aspects of life: professional, personal, spiritual, and physical.
>I am forever a student.
>I listen well and effectively articulate my thoughts.
>I embrace the gifts God has given me and use them with confidence.
>I demonstrate compassion and patience.
>I am not easily offended.
>I acknowledge my failures, inconsistencies, and weaknesses and seek to improve them.
>I will relentlessly seek to be like Jesus.
>I follow this verse: "As for me, I will see Your face in righteousness; / I shall be satisfied when I awake in Your likeness" (Ps. 17:15 NKJV).

Your guiding principles are a collection of things you personally feel passionate about and you want to give greater attention to them. For reasons only completely understood by you and by God, your list will look different from everyone else's and will be a representation of who you feel called to be. Your list may include character qualities you desire to further develop. It may be about spiritual principles you want to focus on, and it may include an important Bible verse or quotation that resonates with who you want to become.

Much as you did when crafting your vision statement, you'll

want to brainstorm your list, edit and rewrite it, review it with trusted friends, and pray over it.

YEARLY GOALS

While your mission statement and guiding principles create a framework to live by, yearly goals help you create specific direction. You may also choose to set five- or ten-year goals for the handful of large items that you are pursuing. Annual goals are meant to get you moving. They give you deadlines and force you to confront fear, complacency, insecurity, or whatever clout killer is holding you back. Without the urgency of these goals, your dreams will remain dreams, and your influence will stagnate. Here are examples of yearly goals:

- Write and publish an article.
- Identify two people to mentor.
- Buy my first home.
- Go on a mission trip.
- Start a family.
- Volunteer more regularly.
- Take a class to further develop a hobby.

Your personal vision statement, guiding principles, and yearly goals become valuable tools in creating the framework to guide how you live out your God-given influence. They keep you on course when you're tempted to be distracted by unforeseen circumstances or when a clout killer is attempting to trip you up.

I'm continually amazed that God desires to partner with us.

I love that he equips us with individual gifts, talents, experiences, and opportunities. I marvel that no two collections look the same. Peter instructed, "Each of you should use whatever gift you have received to serve others, as faithful stewards of God's grace in its various forms" (1 Peter 4:10).

> *Your personal vision statement, guiding principles, and yearly goals become valuable tools in creating the framework to guide how you live out your God-given influence.*

Our God-given influence is a tremendous gift and responsibility, and we have the distinct privilege of partnering with God to bring it to life.

DISCOVERY STEPS

- What experiences has God uniquely given you?
- Do you have a tendency to try to manipulate or control the things that God gives you? How could you live with open hands?
- Take some time to define where you are, where you want to go, and how you're going to get there.

CONCLUSION

Unleashing Your Clout

Be who God meant you to be and you will set the world on fire.

—Catherine of Siena[1]

SEEING SOMEONE LIVE OUT HIS OR HER GIFT always reminds me of the greatness of God. Whether it's a manager motivating a tired and defeated team, an athlete winning his first match, a vocalist wowing an audience, or a brilliant IT person making all the systems run behind the scenes, when someone is living out his clout, he shines. I imagine that God must beam even more brightly and proudly than I do. If I can find such joy in watching people live out their God-given influence, just imagine how significant it must be to him, the God who created us in his own image, the God who begs us to make a careful exploration of who he has created us to be and the work that he has called us to do. When we discover that, when we make sense of it, and then when we start living confidently from that place, nothing could bring him greater joy. Numerous times throughout Scripture he makes a point of saying how much he delights in seeing us do what we're called to do. These particular verses come to mind:

"I know the plans I have for you," declares the LORD, "plans to prosper you and not to harm you, plans to give you hope and a future. Then you will call on me and come and pray to me, and I will listen to you. You will seek me and find me when you seek me with all your heart." (Jer. 29:11–13)

We are God's handiwork, created in Christ Jesus to do good works, which God prepared in advance for us to do. (Eph. 2:10)

Now to him who is able to do immeasurably more than all we ask or imagine, according to his power that is at work within us, to him be glory. (Eph. 3:20–21)

God has equipped you and designed you to live out your unique calling and gifting as a leader. Your heart yearns for influence because it is a part of how he created you. It's God designed, but it can also be humanly distorted when you allow yourself to be derailed by the clout killers we've discussed throughout this book.

Our Galatians passage wraps up with this statement: "Each of you must take responsibility for doing the creative best you can with your own life." I love the hope of this statement. We've wrestled through the clout killers and discussed the dangers of not living out our God-given influence, and we must always remember that there is so much hope and freedom in living the creative best that God designed for us.

So often we get tripped up by the things we are not. We throw excuses at God for why we can't: "I'm not smart enough. I'm not strong enough. I'm not eloquent enough. I don't have the resources. I don't have the privilege. I have too many other responsibilities."

Mary said, "How can this be?" when the angel came to her. Leah lamented, "I am unloved." Rachel exclaimed, "Give me children, or else I die!" Moses asked God, "Who am I that I should go?" and "What if they don't believe me or listen to me?" Peter said, "I will not deny You!" Moses explained, "Because the people come to me to seek God's will."

God has equipped you and designed you to live out your unique calling and gifting as a leader. Your heart yearns for influence because it is a part of how he created you.

We all have excuses or reasons for why we can't be who God is calling us to be, but when we throw aside the excuses and resist our enemies, we begin to see our creative best birthed as we live from our God-given influence.

Whatever the challenge we're facing, we must be aware of the resistance we create for ourselves, often subconsciously. Rather than hold ourselves back, we need to lean in. It's a posture of engagement rather than retreat. It's an attitude of confidence rather than defeat.

What is holding you back? Where do you allow fear, comparison, jealousy, scarcity, insecurity, pride, or control to inhibit you? Where have you become so comfortable with these things that you've become numb to the damage they are doing to your influence?

So often I hear people say that they don't know their calling or purpose; they don't know what God is asking them to do. I trust that through some of the discussions we've had, you've gained more clarity on that. My multitalented friend Bob Goff, who is an author, speaker, and dreamer, simplified it like this: "I think God's hope and plan for us is pretty simple to figure out. For those who resonate with formulas, here it is: add your whole life, your loves, your passions, and your interests together with what God said He wants us to be about, and that's your answer."[2] We make it much more complex than it is.

Look at your life. How have others' expectations, society's norms, your mistakes, and your experiences shaped you? How do you best connect with God, and how can you do that more frequently? What are your spiritual gifts? What talents do you have? What is unique about your personality? How could you best steward all these things that make up who you are? How can you start living your creative best from where you are now? Where do you want to go? What is your personal vision statement? Have you written guiding principles and yearly goals? These questions will get you started. When you confront the crisis of these unanswered questions, your exploration has begun.

WE NEED YOUR CLOUT

Sam was seemingly stuck in a middle-management position at the company where he had worked for nearly a decade. Opportunities for advancement hadn't come his way, and he was beginning to question whether it was time to move on. Expressing his frustration to a coworker one day, he was startled by her response: "Sam, you can't go anywhere! Everyone needs you. Everyone counts on you."

His coworker went on to describe how Sam was known for being the encourager and the backbone of the team. He knew every employee's name and was purposeful in checking in on them, asking about their families and offering a word of encouragement on difficult days. Sam had been completely unaware of how his God-given influence was impacting those around him. Where he equated title and rank with clout, his coworkers measured his influence by how he invested in them. Sam discovered that his God-given influence had very little to do with the position he held and so much more with how he influenced others. His focus became how to love, encourage, and support others while carrying out his work responsibilities.

> *Understanding your God-given influence benefits you and others.*

Understanding your God-given influence benefits you and others. Once you've taken this journey you will begin to live with greater peace and freedom than you've experienced before. Rather than be driven by fear, you will be empowered by love. You will release the unrealistic expectations that you've either placed upon yourself or allowed others to heap upon you. You will find clarity and strength in the unique purpose to which you are called, and you will have a better understanding of how God can use your influence to lead others.

Let me caution you before you become discouraged because you haven't yet experienced this breakthrough of freedom. This breakthrough doesn't occur overnight. It happens gradually. It gets clearer with every exchange you make. It happens when you choose to trade fear for truth, jealousy for encouragement and affirmation, scarcity for generosity, insecurity for love, pride for humility, comparison for focus, and control for trust and faith. You have to look for glimpses of it. You have to stop to identify the moments when you are thriving in your God-given influence.

This clout-cultivating process began to make more sense for me when I realized that I had made all of my life about me. Bound by the fears that kept me anchored to comparison, jealousy, scarcity, insecurity, pride, and control, I didn't recognize that I was consumed with myself. I was worried about what everyone else had and how everyone else perceived me. I thought I was focusing on others, but I was focusing on how others impacted me. It was really all about me. I wasn't operating out of love and concern for others. I was operating with a goal of how to make sure everyone loved me or at least didn't inhibit me. I couldn't see that others were wrestling with all the same enemies that I was. I couldn't fathom that they might be dealing with the same issues.

Recently I attended a conference as one of the speakers. I was excited to meet several of the other speakers there. My insecurity got the best of me, however, and I assumed that since one speaker didn't introduce herself to me, she must not have been interested in meeting me. I gave in to my feelings of insignificance and went about my way. The next day this person reached out via Twitter and said how much she wished we had connected at the conference. I couldn't help laughing at myself. How ridiculously self-focused I had been once again. I assumed it was all about me, but what if she was hoping I would reach out to her? What if she thought I wasn't interested in meeting her since I didn't introduce myself first?

BE FIRST

It's crazy what we can talk ourselves into or out of when we make everything all about us. We miss opportunities for connection and community. We miss the blessing of meeting new friends and making deeper connections. When we allow enemies to impact our influence, we keep our hearts at a distance. Fearful of exposure, we build and maintain walls, and in doing so we keep others at arms' length.

Our God-given influence as leaders can never thrive when we are more worried about our fragile egos than we are about influencing others.

Our God-given influence as leaders can never thrive when we are more worried about our fragile egos than we are about influencing others. What if you went first? What if you made the first introduction, said you were sorry first, admitted a mistake first, or expressed your feelings first?

A statement that has become common is, "Give others the gift of going second." As leaders, we must go first in order to give others the gift of going second. Be the first to be truthful. Be the first to be encouraging. Be the first to affirm someone else. Be the first to be generous. Be the first to be compassionate. Be the first to be humble. Be the first not to compare. Be the first to speak truth. Be the first to display faith.

LEAD FIRST

My husband and I are the proud parents of a fourteen-year-old border collie named Mickey. With no children of our own, all the attention gets diverted to him. He goes everywhere we go and does everything we do. He knows the family routines, and he's quick to tell us if we adjust the schedule too much. People often praise Mick for being the best dog they've ever met. I know I'm biased, but I believe them. He's amazing. But Mick's amazing because he has a great leader.

We rescued Mick eleven years ago from an animal shelter. Living on his own for an undetermined time, Mick was scrawny, scrappy, and very skittish of humans. He wasn't sure how to acclimate to a house with some order and structure. He was a smart dog, but he had no sense of boundaries. Our first few weeks with him were a little dramatic to say the least.

My husband is not one to shy away from a challenge so he dived headfirst into dog psychology to figure out how to best train our new pet. And it didn't take long for my husband to establish the order for our new pack. With tough love and occasional reminders, Mick is well aware that my husband is the pack leader, I am next in line, and Mick brings up the rear. Once my husband established himself as the leader, Mick fell in line. (I, on the other hand, have to be reminded from time to time, but that's a different leadership issue.) Mick values and respects his leader because he knows that my husband is watching out for him. Mick knows that my husband has his best interests at heart, and my husband knows that Mick is counting on him to lead the way.

As leaders, we have the responsibility to go first. We have to run at the front of the pack in order to give others a direction to follow. Don't get lost in the middle of the pack. If you do, you're no longer a leader; you're a follower. In the middle of the pack you lose sight of the vision. In the middle of the pack you succumb to comparison. In the middle of the pack you have trouble seeing the path that needs to be taken. When we give in to our fears, insecurities, jealousy, pride, scarcity, comparisons, or temptation to control, we lose our way and find ourselves surrounded by the herd rather than running ahead. When there is no leader, the people lose their way. "Where there is no vision, the people perish" (Prov. 29:18 KJV).

People are counting on you to lead from your place of influence. God is counting on you to lead from your place of influence. We need you to be you—all of you without holding anything back. Bob Goff pleads with us,

> Despite our inherent beauty, each of us is tempted to hide the original so we won't get damaged. I understand why, I really do. And the fake version of us, it's not worthless. It's just *worth less* because it's only a copy of the real us, a version we don't care about as much. When we hang the fake version out there, it's not the version God created. In that sense, it's like an imposter, a poser, a stunt double is standing in for us and telling the world that this is the best we've got, or the best we'll risk.[3]

Don't hide. We need you. What gift, talent, experience, or opportunity has God given you that you need to explore more? What have you been holding back? God's picture isn't complete without each of us living our creative best. We need you to give all you've got. I'm better when you're better. You're better when I'm better. We're all better together.

CLOUT LIVED OUT

When my crisis of purpose snapped me to attention almost a decade ago, I didn't have a picture of what my future could be once I fully embraced the exploration. Up to that point, most of my life had been motivated by fear, which triggered many of the other clout killers we've discussed. I wasn't thriving in my creative best. I was merely surviving through my fears. There were moments and glimpses of my God-given influence, but they felt too good to be true.

That crisis left me in a place where I could do nothing but take the journey. I had to know. I had to understand what God wanted for my life. I had to understand how he intended to use my gifts and influence. I could no longer be safe and comfortable doing the safe and comfortable. And here's what this journey has taught me about what living our creative best equips us to do:

DREAM BIG

Rather than allow fear to keep us bound by circumstances or perceived inadequacies, when we realize that "if God is for us, who can be against us?" (Rom. 8:31), we quit defining limitations for ourselves and allow God to define the course he intends for us to take. One of my early dreams as a child was to be a writer and a speaker. My version of that dream (precrisis of purpose) allowed me to be comfortable with being the person behind the scenes supporting artists and authors. I felt too small to dream that dream. Only after I made my careful exploration and began to live my creative best did God reignite those dreams with the hope of possibility. You hold in your hands the by-product.

BE UNIQUELY YOU

No pretenses. No fake versions. Thriving in our influence means eliminating comparison and competition. We start to really believe that God intended for us to be unique. As a little girl I used to love the idea that no two snowflakes were the same. This idea confounded me. Born and reared in northern Wisconsin where the average annual snowfall is sixty inches, I had no shortage of snow. The flakes were endless. If God doesn't clone snowflakes, why in the world would he want to replicate one of us? And worse, if he created us with the intention of our being unique, why would he be content with our trying to mimic someone else?

Relax

Our clout enables us to quit freaking out. Jealousy, scarcity, and insecurity quit being parts of our lives. We can let go of the fears that drive us to live in a defensive posture and relax into a heart that is interested in serving, loving, and championing others. We're less threatened and anxious.

Let Go

We can relinquish the pride that keeps us bound by the need to prove ourselves. We have nothing to prove. God has already defined who we are. And we can let go of the control that tries to manipulate the outcomes. Thriving in our creative best gives us the confidence to free-fall into the strong, trustworthy arms of God. We begin to believe that he's got this.

Take Action

Pete Richardson, a life coach and consultant, believes, "Calling once discovered does not just self-activate. . . . There must be a time of ownership [for a calling to be activated]."[4] Upon careful exploration we better understand our part. Our unique gifts, talents, experiences, and opportunities give us perspective on what our God-given influence looks like, and with every step we take in that direction, we become more confident and comfortable moving forward. We no longer have to be paralyzed by the fears that hold us back. We're equipped to move forward confidently.

God wants you to thrive. If you've taken nothing else away from this process, I hope you understand that he longs for you to understand who you are and the work you've been given and then go after it. Sink yourself into it. Do your creative best! When you truly understand how uniquely God has designed you and how specifically he has equipped you, you will thrive. The clout killers will lose their hold, and the replacements will break through. Paul pleaded with each of us, "I urge you to live a life worthy of the calling you have received" (Eph. 4:1). I urge you to do the same.

> *When you truly understand how uniquely God has designed you and how specifically he has equipped you, you will thrive.*

Your God-given influence is a gift to you and others. We need you to thrive so that you can help others thrive. This journey, although painful at times, is part of what equips you to be the leader God has called you to be. Parker Palmer reminds us that "good leadership comes from people who have penetrated their own inner darkness and arrived at the place where we are at one with one another, people who can lead the rest of us to a place of 'hidden wholeness' because they have been there and know the way."[5] Although our journey may have forced you to face dark parts of your leadership, I pray the exploration has been worth the effort. I'm praying you will embrace and live out your God-given influence—your clout!

DISCOVERY STEPS

- Where do you see glimpses of your God-given influence?
- Which clout killers are the most troublesome for you? What steps can you take to begin replacing them?
- Where do you need to go first and lead the way for others when it comes to living out your God-given influence?

ACKNOWLEDGMENTS

TO THE AMAZING PEOPLE WHO WERE WILLING TO RISK THEIR clout to support mine:

Tami Heim, thank you for mapping out this concept with me over numerous cups of tea. Your belief and enthusiasm were the loving antidotes to my raging insecurities!

Shannon Litton, thank you for picking up the torch and never missing a step. You get me. I'm so grateful!

Kat Davis, thank you for being a constant example of how to live generously. You challenge my scarcity tendencies, not with your words but by your example. Thank you for making such valuable connections.

Amy Hiett, I know this book would have never made it to Patrick's desk without your belief. Thank you for championing it!

Patrick Lencioni, thank you is not nearly enough. I'm honored and humbled that you would lend your voice in support of this book. You are a clout cultivator!

Jenny Black, you instigated this journey. Thank you for following a prompting from God to reach out to me.

The amazing team at Thomas Nelson. Brian Hampton, thank you for believing in the vision and giving this message a chance. Bryan Norman, your influence brought this book to life. Thank you for leading me through this process with such kindness and candor. Your clout speaks loudly through these pages. Angela Scheff, thank you for being one of the first to believe in this manuscript. Your belief in me is a gift. Janene MacIvor, thank you for guiding me so wonderfully through the details. Chad Cannon and Katy Boatman, thank you for allowing me to tap a little bit of my marketing roots to dream about possibilities. Tiffany Sawyer, thank you for connecting with this project so quickly. Tom Knight and the entire sales team, I know your job can be relentless. Thank you for sharing this book with passion and commitment.

Cross Point team, you seriously are the best staff on earth! Thank you for enduring the bruises of my undeveloped clout.

Family, friends, and mentors who speak continuous encouragement and wisdom in my life: Dad, Hilda, Pete and Brandi Wilson, Ashley Warren, Annie Downs, Margaret Feinberg, Jeff Henderson, the Goldens, Sarah Atkinson, Stephen Brewster, Katie Strandlund, Lindsey Nobles, and to everyone who has read my blog posts, listened to me speak, or allowed me to ramble about leadership, thank you for indulging my passion.

To the creator of my clout, dear Jesus, I'm grateful . . . so truly grateful!

RESOURCES

Spiritual Gifts Assessment

Lifechurch.tv provides a free Spiritual Gifts assessment on their church resource site. Go to http://open .lifechurch.tv/ to create an account and access this great resource.

StrengthsFinder Assessment

The StrengthsFinder Assessment is available for a nominal fee on the Gallup Strengths Center website: https://www.gallupstrengthscenter.com/.

Additional Personality Tests

There are a number of great tests that may be helpful in better understanding your personality.

- DISC Profile: http://www.discprofile.com/
- Enneagram: https://www.enneagraminstitute.com/
- Myers-Briggs: http://www.myersbriggs.org/

BOOKS

S.H.A.P.E.: Finding and Fulfilling Your Unique Purpose for Life by Erik Rees

Now, Discover Your Strengths by Marcus Buckingham and Donald O. Clifton

StrengthsFinder 2.0 by Tom Rath

NOTES

INTRODUCTION: YOU HAVE "IT"

1. John Maxwell, *Ultimate Leadership* (Nashville: Thomas Nelson, 2007).

CHAPTER 1: YOU DON'T HAVE TO BE AFRAID

1. Mark Twain. (n.d.). BrainyQuote.com. Retrieved May 31, 2013, from BrainyQuote.com Web site: http://www.brainyquote.com/quotes/quotes/m /marktwain138540.html.

2. Susan Jeffers, *Feel the Fear . . . and Do It Anyway: Dynamic Techniques for Turning Fear, Indecision, and Anger into Power, Action, and Love* (New York: Fawcett, 1987), 14.

3. Ibid., emphasis in original.

4. Ibid., 15–16.

5. Ibid., 15.

6. John Kenneth Galbraith quoted from his *Age of Uncertainty* (1977), in *Bill Clinton: The Inside Story* by Robert E. Levin (New York: S.P.I. Books, 1993), 246.

7. Sarah Young, *Jesus Calling* (Nashville: Thomas Nelson, 2004), 5.

8. Lynne Hybels, *Nice Girls Don't Change the World* (Grand Rapids: Zondervan, 2005), 76.

9. Parker J. Palmer, *Let Your Life Speak* (San Francisco: Jossey-Bass, 2000), 93–94, emphasis in original.

10. Max Lucado, *Fearless* (Nashville: Thomas Nelson, 2009), 215.

CHAPTER 2: YOU MORE THAN MEASURE UP

1. Marcus Aurelius, *Meditations* (Hollywood, FL: Simon & Brown, 2012), 25.

2. From Robert Morris's message "The Sin of Comparison," http://www.youtube.com /watch?v=EfADMTJ0GIE.

3. Ibid.

4. Tony Morgan, "Stop & Start 2012: Jeff Henderson," Tony Morgan Live, (blog), January 24, 2012, http:// tonymorganlive.com/2012/01/24/stop-start-2012 -jeff-henderson/.

5. W. Chan Kim and Renée Mauborgne, *Blue Ocean Strategy* (Boston: Harvard Business School Publishing, 2005), x.

6. David E. C. Huggins, *The Elegant Strategist* (Morriston, Ontario, Canada: Andros Consultants, 2003), 259–60.

CHAPTER 3: YOU ARE ENOUGH

1. Antisthenes cited in *Dictionary of Quotations*
   (Classical), ed. Thomas Benfield Harbottle (New
   York: Macmillan, 1906), 542.
2. Tanya Menon and Leigh Thompson, "Envy at
   Work," *Harvard Business Review* 88 (April 2010): 3.
3. Ibid., 2.
4. John Tierney, "Envy May Bear Fruit, but It Also Has
   an Aftertaste," *New York Times*, October 10, 2011,
   http://www.nytimes.com/2011/10/11/science
   /11tierney.html?pagewanted=all&_r=0.
5. Robert Morris's message "The Sin of Comparison,"
   May 28, 2011, http://www.youtube.com/watch?v
   =EfADMTJ0GIE.
6. Nancy Beach, *Gifted to Lead* (Grand Rapids:
   Zondervan, 2008), 157.

CHAPTER 4: YOU HAVE ENOUGH

1. Stephen R. Covey, *Principle-Centered Leadership*
   (New York: Fireside, 1991), 158.
2. Brené Brown, *Daring Greatly: How the Courage to Be
   Vulnerable Transforms the Way We Live, Love, Parent,
   and Lead* (New York: Gotham Books, 2012), 28.
3. Susan Jeffers, *Feel the Fear . . . and Do It Anyway:
   Dynamic Techniques for Turning Fear, Indecision,
   and Anger into Power, Action, and Love* (New York:
   Fawcett, 1987), 170.
4. American Psychological Association, "Stress in

the Workplace: Survey Summary," March 2011, 2, http://www.apa.org/news/press/releases/phwa -survey-summary.pdf.

5. Douglas LaBier, "The New Resilience: The Lowdown on Abusive Bosses and the Unhealthy Workplace—Part 1," *Psychology Today*, June 25, 2011, http://www.psychologytoday.com/blog/the -new-resilience/201106/the-lowdown-abusive -bosses-and-the-unhealthy-workplace-part-1.

6. David Allen, *Getting Things Done: The Art of Stress- Free Productivity* (New York: Penguin, 2001), 4–5.

7. John C. Maxwell, *The 21 Most Powerful Minutes in a Leader's Day* (Nashville: Thomas Nelson, 2000), 205.

8. Erika Andersen, "Generous Leaders Aren't Naive– They're Confident," *Forbes*, July 30, 2012, http:// www.forbes.com/sites/erikaandersen/2012/07/30 /generous-leaders-arent-naive-theyre-confident/.

CHAPTER 5: YOU ARE GOOD ENOUGH

1. "Vin Diesel: I Want to Be a Good Dad," *Parade*, August 25, 2008, http://www.parade.com/celebrity /celebrity-parade/archive/pc_0230.html.

2. Joseph Nowinski, *The Tender Heart: Conquering Your Insecurity* (New York: Fireside, 2001), 23.

3. John C. Maxwell, "Insecurity: Leadership Flaw of America's Worst President," *Philippine Daily Inquirer*, November 3, 2012, http://business.inquirer .net/90968/insecurity-leadership-flaw-of-americas -worst-president.

4. Beth Moore, *So Long, Insecurity* (Carol Stream, IL: Tyndale House, 2010), 27, emphasis in original.

CHAPTER 6: YOU DON'T HAVE TO KNOW IT ALL

1. Mother Teresa, *No Greater Love* (Novato, CA: New World Library, 2001), 55.

2. *Merriam-Webster's Collegiate Dictionary*, 11th ed., s.v. "pride."

3. Ken Blanchard and Scott Blanchard, "Don't Let Your Ego Hijack Your Leadership Effectiveness," *Fast Company*, June 22, 2012, http://www.fastcompany .com/1840932/dont-let-your-ego-hijack-your-leadership -effectiveness.

4. Sarah Young, *Jesus Calling* (Nashville: Thomas Nelson, 2004), 136.

5. Joel Manby, *Love Works: Seven Timeless Principles for Effective Leaders* (Grand Rapids: Zondervan, 2012), 174–75.

6. Ibid., 175.

7. Ibid., 22.

8. Parker J. Palmer, *Let Your Life Speak* (San Francisco: Jossey-Bass, 2000), 70.

9. Rick Warren, Twitter post, April 19, 2011, 7:32 p.m., http://twitter.com/RickWarren.

10. Doug Guthrie and Sudhir Venkatesh, "Creative Leadership: Humility and Being Wrong," *Forbes*, June 1, 2012, http://www.forbes.com/sites /dougguthrie/2012/06/01/creative-leadership -humility-and-being-wrong/.

Chapter 7: You Can Let Go

1. Henri Nouwen cited in *The Control Freak* by Les Parrott III (Carol Stream, IL: Tyndale House, 2000), 21.

2. Lord Acton Quote Archive, Acton Institute, http://www.acton.org/research/lord-acton-quote-archive.

3. *Merriam-Webster's Collegiate Dictionary*, 11th ed., s.v. "control freak."

4. Parrott, *The Control Freak*, 2.

5. Elliot D. Cohen, "What Would Aristotle Do?" *Psychology Today*, May 22, 2011, http://www.psychologytoday.com/blog/what-would-aristotle-do/201105/the-fear-losing-control.

6. Parrott, *The Control Freak*, 48.

7. Brené Brown cited in "Why Doing Awesome Work Means Making Yourself Vulnerable," by Drake Baer, *Fast Company*, September 17, 2012, http://www.fastcompany.com/3001319/why-doing-awesome-work-means-making-yourself-vulnerable.

8. Cohen, "What Would Aristotle Do?"; emphasis in original.

9. Bill Hybels, *Holy Discontent* (Grand Rapids: Zondervan, 2007), http://zondervan.com/9780310272281.

10. John C. Maxwell, *The Maxwell Leadership Bible* (Nashville: Thomas Nelson, 2002), 769, emphasis in original.

CHAPTER 8: DISCOVERING YOUR IDENTITY

1. Dallas Willard, *The Divine Conspiracy* (New York: HarperCollins, 1997), 15.

2. Jonathan Aitken, *John Newton: From Disgrace to Amazing Grace* (Wheaton, IL: Crossway Books, 2007), 53.

3. For more information about Keating's levels of awareness, see Cynthia Bourgeault, *Mystical Hope: Trusting in the Mercy of God* (Lanham, MD: Rowman & Littlefield, 2001).

4. Shirley S. Wang, "Under the Influence: How the Group Changes What We Think," *Wall Street Journal*, May 3, 2011, http://online.wsj.com/article /SB10001424052748704436004576298962165925364 .html.

5. *The Dave Ramsey Show*, http://www.daveramsey .com/radio/about-dave/.

6. Dave Ramsey's company, the Lampo Group, Inc., http://www.daveramsey.com/company.

7. Ibid.

8. Ruth Haley Barton, *Strengthening the Soul of Your Leadership* (Downers Grove, IL: InterVarsity Press, 2008), 31.

CHAPTER 9: DEVELOPING YOUR CONFIDENCE

1. Alan Hirsch and Debra Hirsch, *Untamed* (Grand Rapids: Baker Books, 2010), 182.

2. Dr. and Mrs. Howard Taylor, *Hudson Taylor's Spiritual Secret* (Chicago: Moody Bible Institute, 2009), 239.

CHAPTER 10: DEFINING YOUR MISSION

1. Robin Gerber: *Leadership the Eleanor Roosevelt Way* (New York: Penguin, 2002), 63.

2. Joel Manby, *Love Works: Seven Timeless Principles for Effective Leaders* (Grand Rapids: Zondervan, 2012), 178–79.

3. Ibid., 179–80, emphasis in original.

4. See Gary Chapman, *The 5 Love Languages* (Grand Rapids: Zondervan, 2010); the languages are words of affirmation, quality time, gifts, acts of service, and physical touch.

5. See Marcus Buckingham and Donald O. Clifton, *Now, Discover Your Strengths* (New York: Free Press, 2001).

6. *Merriam-Webster's Collegiate Dictionary*, 11th ed., s.v. "pleasure."

CHAPTER 11: DETERMINING YOUR PASSION

1. George Bernard Shaw, *Man and Superman* (New York: Penguin, 2000), 165, in a speech by the character Don Juan.

2. PowerPoint presentation, http://www.ppt2txt.com/r /7391fe68/.

Conclusion: Unleashing Your Clout

1. Catherine of Siena cited in *Queen Elizabeth II and Her Church* by John Hall (London: Bloomsbury Publishing, 2012), 152.

2. Bob Goff, *Love Does* (Nashville: Thomas Nelson, 2012), 143.

3. Ibid., 149, emphasis in original.

4. Pete Richardson, "Find Your Calling," Q: Ideas for the Common Good, http://www.qideas.org/video /calling.aspx.

5. Parker J. Palmer, *Let Your Life Speak* (San Francisco: Jossey-Bass, 2000), 80–81.

ABOUT THE AUTHOR

JENNI CATRON SERVES AS THE EXECUTIVE DIREC-
tor of Cross Point Church in Nashville, Tennessee. She leads the
staff of Cross Point and oversees the ministry of its five cam-
puses. Before joining the staff of Cross Point, she worked in artist
development in the Christian music industry for nine years.

Jenni's passion is to lead well and to inspire, equip, and
encourage others to do the same. She speaks at conferences
and churches nationwide, seeking to help others develop their
leadership gifts and lead confidently in the different spheres of
influence that God has granted them. Jenni blogs at www.jenni
catron.com and contributes to other online publications.

Jenni loves having a fabulous cup of tea, reading great
books, learning the game of tennis, and hanging out with her
husband and their border collie.